D0338474

NEALE DONALD WALSCH
and
DR. BRAD BLANTON

Honest to God

A Change of Heart
That Can Change the World

Published by:
Sparrowhawk Publications
646 Shuler Lane
Stanley, VA 22851
800 EL TRUTH
www.radicalhonesty.com

Distributed by:
Hampton Roads Publishing
1125 Stony Ridge Road
Charlottesville, VA 22902
Orders: 800 766 8009

Produced by Authors Publishing Cooperative
Cover by Vicki Valentine
Cover photo of Neale Donald Walsch ©Christopher Briscoe
Interior Design by Art Squad Graphics
Printed in Canada
First Edition

10 9 8 7 6 5 4 3 2 1

Table of Contents

Foreword

"The truth shall set you free" — John 8:32

Remarkable things happen when people become open and honest. Incredible things happen when they do it all the time.

Almost everyone agrees about that. Hardly anyone seems to know what to do about it, however. This book discusses what can be done about it.

No one else is really talking about this. Not in this direct a way. Not with the head-on approach that you are going to find here. Some will also see this as a dangerous book, because it will threaten their way of life, and all the societal institutions that are in place to support it.

And what is so threatening here? Just what is so *threatening?*

The message of this book, which, after all is said and done, breaks down to six words:

LET'S ALL JUST BE HONEST.

That message could change your life. It could also change the world.

That's what some people are worried about.

Not all people. Just some people. Mainly people who would have a lot to lose if the world *did* change.

Mostly, these are the people who hold power, and who think that they need to hold power in order to be happy. And not just hold power, but hold it in a particular way. Namely, power *over*, not power *with.*

People who are willing to hold power with others have no problem with the idea of total honesty. Only people who want to hold power over others have difficulty with this concept. These people are in the minority.

Most people are intrigued by the idea of transparency and complete honesty in relationships—a way of being that for the purposes of this discussion we shall call *radical honesty.* Brad has written a book by that title that has touched hundreds of thousands, and Neale has talked about *transparency* and *total visibility* as a lifestyle in his best-selling "Conversations with God" books read by millions of people. So we both have the same message to send, and we've chosen to join forces to send it.

Why? Because people are scared. Even as they are intrigued, they are also a bit scared. The people who want to have power over them have made them scared. They've told dire stories about what happens when the truth, the whole truth, and nothing but the truth is told, and they've spread the word that this is to be avoided at all cost. Indeed, the power structure in our society actually rewards those who do not tell the truth, and punishes those who do. Why do you suppose that people lie all the time?

Nobody tells the truth about anything any more. Not anything important. Everybody's lying to everybody else, and everybody knows it. It was once our dirty little secret and now it's not even dirty any more because it's become so common that it's now the truth tellers who are the dirty ones. It's the whistle blowers and the truth tellers who are criticized, and the totally honest person who is held up as an example of socially unacceptable behavior.

So people are now scared to be honest. After centuries of this training they are caught in a trap of their own devise, yet live in fear of the very thing that will set them free. Truth heals, and they think that it is the truth that hurts.

At a lecture Neale delivered in Boston in which he talked about "utter transparency as a lifestyle," a member of the audience became quite agitated. "Does that mean," he asked, "the truth, the whole truth and nothing but the truth, no matter how much it hurts someone else?"

We'll begin our exploration of this dynamite topic here, because this is where the rubber meets the road. And as we undertake our exploration, we'll warn you that we may use some words here that may make you blush. We may say some things here that may cause you discomfort. And we may propose some solutions here that may send you screaming into the night, that "These guys are crazy."

Maybe it is crazy to think that most of what's going wrong on this planet (and in our personal lives) could be set right by the use of one single tool: the truth. On the other hand, maybe those who are telling you not to tell the truth (not directly, of course, but indirectly, by their behaviors) are the crazies. Insanity has been defined as doing the same thing over and over again, expecting to get a different outcome. We've been lying to each other and lying to ourselves for centuries now and it hasn't worked. Still, we keep doing it, and we're encouraged to keep doing it by a society that doesn't know any other way.

Our politicians, in their attempts to win approval from everyone and offend no one, just don't know any other way.

Our businesses, in their desperate competitions with each other, just don't know any other way.

Our schools, in their reflections of the decisions and values of the society in which they exist, just don't know any other way.

Even our religions, in their maniacal drive to convince everyone that their way is the only way to God, just don't know any other way.

And so, with all of our institutions modeling the lying behavior, we are taught to lie and to support others in lying. We lie to each other now, about the smallest things. Forget about the big things; they went by the wayside a long time ago. We are now deep into the era of the Social Lie. We won't even tell the truth about why we don't choose to play bridge tonight.

There's a way out of this, and it's total transparency. It's radical honesty. And it works. It changes everything. It empowers, it does not disempower. It heals, it does not damage. It is focused on intimacy. True intimacy, the kind based on sharing the way your life actually is. Not Hollywood romance. Not pleasantness like in the movie "Pleasantville."

Not those things. It is an acknowledgement of the truth of our experience as it actually is, without build up or spin or distortion of any kind. It is the love of what is so. It is the love of being itself that allows us to love and honor other beings with the truth.

It may look, as you begin reading this book, as though it has nothing to do with the present global crisis. Only deep insight and a willingness to see what most of us have been unwilling to see about ourselves will cause you to notice how extraordinarily relevant the following words are to what is now occurring on the planet. So, for those of you who see the relevancy, there will be great rewards. We invite you to turn this page and to write a new chapter in the history of the human race.

Neale Donald Walsch and Brad Blanton
November, 2001

1

Introduction:

The Democratic Unconvention

We're going to talk about the power of honesty in an unusual way. So not only is this book going to be unusual for its content, but for the way its content is presented. We're going to do something that authors are "not allowed" to do. We're going to mix conventions in this book.

A convention is the way a book is constructed. If a book is written entirely in the first person, for instance, that's a convention. The dialogue that Neale used in "Conversations with God" could be called a convention. It is what actually happened, but the fact that he presented the material he received this way would be called, in literary terms, a convention.

In this book we are going to mix conventions. Some of the book is written as a single-voice narrative. As a reader, you know that the book is written by both of us, and so the convention is that both of us are saying every word. The truth is that one of us wrote some of the words and the other of us wrote other words and both of us have read the words and agree with them, or modified them and then both agreed. And the whole truth is that most of the words were written by neither of us.

That's right. Neither of us wrote most of the words in this book. We said them. To each other.

This book is taken from a dialogue that we had in front of television cameras for several hours in a hotel room in Boston. We'd decided that we wanted to get together and do this television taping of our views, ideas, questions and commentaries on the whole issue of telling the truth, becoming totally transparent and radically honest. That taping went extremely well and out of it came not only a video program, but an audio program as well, because we simply lifted the audio track and put it on a cassette tape.

And now what we've done is have a stenographer transcribe the dialogue and we've read it line by line and then added more of our own written comments in order to expand on the dialogue, and now we've turned all of that into this book.

And here's where the mixed convention comes in. There are times when the actual exchange of comments between us in the original dialogue is, we think, more stimulating (and simply more fun to read) than a continuously running single-voice narrative. There are also times when we don't necessarily agree with every word that is spoken by the other. So we've broken the narrative into its original two-person dialogue now and then, when doing so preserved the sparkle and the intent, the nuance and the flavor and, importantly, the identity and ownership of the more personal of our views. We've also taken the slight liberty of updating a few of the past-tense references in the dialogue, to keep it current.

We use "BB" to indicate the words spoken by Brad Blanton and "NDW" to indicate the words spoken by Neale Donald Walsch when we do this. We hope you won't let the switching back and forth from one convention into another throw you. In fact, we hope that you'll find it just "different" enough from other books to make this an even more exciting and engaging read.

There is a second somewhat unconventional convention in the way we have presented the content of this book. It's this: part one of this book is about personal transformation through honesty, about how the first jail you have to get out of is in your own mind. Part two is about how the truth can set you free (how it manifests in personal, family, and relationship life). Then part three is about social transformation through honesty (how lying manifests in the current social order), and how honesty might manifest itself to bring about needed social change. Finally, in part four you get our analysis of how lying harms and honesty heals in the wider social realm and what that has to do with our world today, after the events of September 11, 2001.

At the end, in the postscript, we come full circle; to speak about the leadership function of personal honesty to bring about much needed social change in current times.

This structure for the book came about as the book evolved and as our society evolved. The tragic events of September 11, 2001 happened as we were almost ready to go to press. We met and talked and were both struck by how the book we were about to release to the world was extremely relevant to this new world we all now live in, where a certain level of safety can no longer be presumed. We decided to make explicit the relationship between what we have learned about honesty and both personal and social change, using current events as a clear example of the need for a greater honesty.

One thing that gives us hope for the world is something we have found to be true about the human spirit. There is a courage and survivability that human beings have. It's as though the life force is simply stronger, when all is said and done, than the forces of tragedy. Whether we're talking about personal psychological change or social psychological change, a manifestation of the human spirit recurs over and over again and demands to be acknowledged.

When an individual or couple undergo an intense personal tragedy, like the loss of a child or the unanticipated death of a family member, the process of grieving and adapting to the loss, sometimes, and we would say, often, manifests as a positive change in the way of living for the person. That change, in the long run, turns out to be a critical turning point with positive results in that person's life. A friend said to one of us just the other day. "I still wish my husband had not been taken from me, but because of all I've learned through that loss—about myself and about the kindness of others and about life itself, I wouldn't trade that experience for anything." There is clearly often a transformation through suffering on the personal level. We also know from our own living history that mutually suffered loss, as in the Depression, or World War II, or the death of President Kennedy, or the assassination of Martin Luther King—out of these sufferings, positive social transformation has come.

We deeply wish to see the emergence of a positive transformation through the suffering that comes from the terrorist attacks on the World Trade Center and the Pentagon, and our responses to them. We pray a better world emerges out of what we learn from that suffering, and we offer the last section of this book as a beginning toward that end.

So now, let's talk about intimacy, and about transparency, and about radical honesty.

PART I

Personal Transformation

Through Honesty

2

Intimacy

It is true that in order to achieve intimacy it is sometimes necessary to risk offending people, or hurting their feelings. Brad has been a clinical psychologist for over 25 years, and has given "Radical Honesty" workshops and retreats for the past twelve years. What he coaches people to do is to *stay with* others if they get hurt or offended until they feel their way through it and get over it.

Don't do a drive-by. Don't run in there and share a bunch of resentments or things that hurt people's feelings, and then cut out. Instead say, "I'm here. I'm here to talk to you, to forgive you. What I need to do to forgive you is to tell you the truth about my judgments about you, about my resentments of you and about my appreciations of you. Then I can Experience the experience of being in contact with you and in touch with what I feel about you at the same time. And whenever I can do that I will be able to forgive you and it will benefit me, and I want you to bear with me in this conversation until we get to that place where we've forgiven each other."

Often others don't feel like there's any reason for you to have to forgive them. Their instant reaction may be to say, "Wait a minute! I don't think you have any cause to forgive me. I've done nothing to you. You're doing it all to yourself."

That, of course, is absolutely true. It's our own unmet expectations that are the source of our anger, and when we say that others have violated our expectations, it's we who make that judgment and we who are attached to that judgment. Philosophically, there is no disagreement with the person who might say this. *Process-wise, however, you can't reach a conclusion with your mind, and accomplish with your psyche the conclusion that your mind has reached,* unless you go through the process of *contacting* the other person and *telling the truth and being in touch with your own experience while you're in touch with them.* That's what allows forgiveness to occur and, yes, sometimes forgiveness is a hard process.

There is a sort of spiritual narcissism model of forgiveness we are not talking about. We don't mean a Marin County, California, pie-in-the-sky, Miller High Life, elitism of the in-group, la la land spirituality, where everything is easy and if-we-just-all-love-each-other-everything-will-turn-out-fine-sweetie-just-don't-worry-about-it. We're not talking about that. We are talking about getting over things in real life, in real human interactions, by being honest and feeling your way through to forgiveness. You do this by sharing how your life really is with other people who may be temporarily your enemy.

Brad is now working on a book called "The Truth Tellers: Stories of Success by Honest People." The stories are coming in. These are stories of people who went back and saw their parents and played the videotape of their life story, which they made in the eight-day workshop called "The Course in Honesty." In this setting they get an hour to tell the whole story of their life to a group of peers. Then they are asked to take that and show it to their parents, or spouses, or siblings and have a conversation with them about it.

It's a fabulous process, and the participants know before they tell their story that they're going to be asked to show the tape to their parents, and they're always in charge of doing it or not doing it. When they tell their story in the context of a community of friends who have promised each other to be completely honest, what gets on the tape is not quite the same as the usual "pitch" most people give their parents.

Often when they do watch the tape with their families, their parents say, "Well, that's not what happened at all," or their brothers or sisters say, "That's not the way I remember it," or "I don't know where you got that," or "It hurts my feelings that you said that." That's when the workshop participants remember that they were asked to stay with those to whom they have revealed the truth about their version of history beyond the initial reaction, and then continue with the conversation. Their parents and brothers and sisters and friends and ex-husbands and wives have their own resentments and their own versions of what occurred. Sometimes quite animated conversations arise.

What they tell us about these conversations is that they transform the whole family. And in a really positive way. People discover that they really do love each other and love is not an act to be maintained but an *actual real experience of warmth and excitement*. And *words that reveal* bring it about. And words that *conceal* prevent it from happening. The conversation keeps going the next Thanksgiving and then Christmas, and then Easter and the Thanksgiving after that. It's really the beginning of a new conversation about *what life really is for* them, because the deeper level they reached goes beyond the superficiality of their traditional "normal" family interactions.

Fear of the Intensity of Feelings

Have you ever wondered why people spend years—not weeks or months, but thirty, forty, fifty *years*—in superficiality? What that's about? And what are they afraid of?

They're afraid of feelings themselves.

Most of us are. There's something about intensity of feelings, per se. There's a certain avoidance of that level of sensation itself. We usually go to the level of emotional interpretation and try to "understand" our feelings as a way of avoiding having the feelings at the level of sensation in our body. The level of emotional interpretation is actually more removed from experience than the level of sensation.

For instance, let's take a look at anger. Anger is nothing more than a set of sensations in the body. It's a tightening up of the whole body, a shortness of breath, a more-rapid heartbeat, tension across the back, etc. They're just that—merely sensations, and nothing more. And if you're willing to experience those sensations, you'll discover that they come and they go away, as all sensations do. Yet most people are not ready to make that discovery. They're afraid to live at the place where life is just "sensational." They think that they're going to get hurt, and so they seek protection in a belief system. Some people would rather have an interpretation of reality than reality itself.

John Bradshaw said that if you get a bunch of co-dependent people and march them down a hallway, and one door says "HEAVEN" above it and the second door says "CONVERSATIONS ABOUT HEAVEN," they'll all go through the second door. They would rather just talk about it.

When did we as a race, as a species, make this cultural decision that we would rather have the story than the experience? Did we as a culture ever make that a conscious decision? Perhaps not. It might have been just a process that developed over a long period of time. Self-protection, or self-survival became self-image protection and self- image survival. It may be instinctual, just to avoid pain. It may be a natural extension of that instinct to avoid predicted damage to one's ego. Someone said that all of life is an effort to avoid discomfort and displeasure.

This self-image protection may have evolved because human beings seem to sense the danger from other human beings. It may not be the evolution of man with nature as much as man with man, because human beings have found each other to be dangerous creatures.

In a book called "The Third Chimpanzee," written by a sociobiologist named Jared Diamond, the author looks at humans and their first cousins to try to figure out how exactly we differ. Diamond is trying to correlate what we've found out by breaking the genetic code with the archeological and anthropological record of human history. He went back and studied what happened in the caves among human beings, and he also looked at the evolution of the genetic structure. Diamond finds that our closest cousin is the chimpanzee, because we have exactly 98.6% of the same genetic material, and therefore much difference between chimpanzees and human beings, genetically speaking.

So where is the difference? Chimpanzees do sex a little differently, and this is probably the source of many of the major differences between us.

When the female chimpanzee goes into heat she emits a dull musky odor, and her body changes in shape and in color, which attracts the males. The first five or six strongest male chimps fight the other ones off and have sex with her. Then, when she goes out of heat, they're not interested anymore.

Diamond says that these changes in the female during estrus are called a "display" and that this is very common in nature. Either the male or female goes into a "display period" that calls forth a response from the opposite sex. What happened to us, about 500,000 or so years ago, is that our females went into permanent display. Their rounded breasts and buttocks appeal constantly to the males. Instead of sex just during ovulation as it is for our chimpanzee cousins, impregnation occurs from basically the male and female having sex whenever the opportunity for it arises. This way, there is often some sperm present when the egg comes down the tube. Though this is a minor change in sexual reproductive strategy it has far-ranging social implications. The males are constantly called forth without any relief and the women are constantly called upon for sex. There's this level of testosterone in us that comes up and stays constant, causing more fighting and aggression. This may be what helped cause the evolution of the mind. It was probably a significant factor in what also made us the meanest species the planet has ever seen.

We're also the most merciless species. We obliterated the woolly mammoth in a mere 11,000 years or so while coming from the Bering Straight down to the tip of South America. We killed off all the woolly mammoths by killing one off every time we wanted to have a steak and leaving the rest of it lay there to rot. Human beings will do that.

But it isn't just animals that we kill. Human beings wipe out whole groups of their own species. In recent times, the invasion of America and Australia and the subsequent decimation of the native populations, Nazi Germany, Kosovo, and the present day terrorist attacks and their aftermath are all only the latest verse of a very old song. Once a human being can categorize another human being as the "enemy," they can do anything to them they want. They can kill all the women, the children, pets, slaves and anything else living that happens to be around. As long as one group of us considers ourselves better than our neighbors, the others become fair game. Now, with a world population of over six billion as a result of this comparatively very successful sexual reproduction strategy (there are not that many chimpanzees), the question of how to control this tendency for violence has become critical. We must now ask, "How can we save an endangered planet from ourselves?"

Putting an End to "Better"

What will save the planet is when we bring an end to "better." An end to the idea that we are somehow better than another class of people. That is the new gospel that was written by Neale in "Friendship with God." He asked in his dialogue, "If there were one single thing,"—and it's a huge question—"if there were one single thing we could do to resolve the conflicts, or at least lower the level of negative interactions with each other, what would it be?" The answer came back so fast. Just bring an end to "better," bring an end to the idea of superiority—that you are somehow the "chosen people," or "one nation under God," or "doing the will of Allah," or whoever you think you are being or doing that makes you more special than the next group—because your idea of "betterness" or "specialness" is, in fact, what gives you justification to treat everyone the way you treat them.

If you thought that others were exactly the same as you and that neither one of you were any better and, furthermore, if you thought that they *were* you—an extension *of* you—if you got that "we are all One," then all of that would automatically disappear.

The Sufis talk about what they call the Holy Human Prototype. It's when I'm looking at you and you're looking at me and I notice that the set of eyes over there is pretty much like the set of eyes I see when I look in the mirror. I salute, saying, "Hello, fellow being." So there's this Being over there and there's this Being over here. That's what Sufis call the Holy Human Prototype. One HHP acknowledges another, "Hello." That's what they say love is. And that's what they say is the basis of the end of war, the acknowledgement of one Holy Human Prototype to another.

The question before the human race is, why can't we get to that? Not just the end of war between nations, but the end of war over the dinner table. What stops us from getting to that?

The answer is that our minds are not always our best servant. We've been raised in our culture to have a lot of faith in our minds. There's a saying in Brad's books . . . "The mind is a terrible thing. Waste it."

The Being notices things and the Mind thinks things. The two are not the same. Now in order to acknowledge other human beings as equal to you—to say "I'm equal as a being to you, you're equal as a being to me, and so is every other being"—we have to *Notice*. Noticing is an experience that comes from paying attention to another. Noticing is distinct from thinking. Thinking is when you go off into your categories about your experience of being, and noticing is when you're being God-like, what the Sufis call acknowledging the Holy Human Prototype, acknowledging the godhood in your fellow man.

People like to *think* instead of *notice* because they believe they are in charge of their thoughts and therefore can have some control of themselves and others through thinking. Of course, that is an illusion as well, but a highly valued one. People feel "safe" by thinking they are in charge of their lives by thinking.

But what the mind goes into when it thinks is fear. And the mind goes into fear because it is *imagining* things based on only partially conscious memories of previous experience, rather than *experiencing* what is going on right now. If you acknowledge all others as your equal at the level of being, it is a scary thing for the mind. The mind doesn't like that, given that it likes to think of itself as special and that who you are *is* your mind, rather than a *being* with a mind.

So we imagine that it is not going to be good for us to simply acknowledge what we notice. It is not going to be good for our government, it is not going to be good for our economy, it is not going to be good for our religion or our relationships or any part of how we live our life. This is what we *imagine*, because this is what we have been told a lot by other scared people.

If we paid attention to our *feelings* more than our *minds* we may find that our identification with the *being* we are and the *being of other people* would have power over our minds. That would be problematic in a lot of ways. We would do what our hearts told us. We would employ our minds in service to our beings. We wouldn't be able to predict what was about to happen as well because we couldn't know in advance.

We have all been warned repeatedly against compassion being the organizing principle of our lives. And for good reason. It is a threat to our familiar way of life.

Remembering is merely another form of imagining. It is imagining that what once happened is what is going to happen now. You have been told this by those who want to exercise power *over* you, not *with* you. And they have also created actual happenings and occurrences in accordance with this message, so that you will not forget it. Your teachers and parents taught you to be paranoid and guarded for your own good.

But imagining from the past, or imagining from what you have been told, is not the same as experiencing what is going on right here, right now. We (that is, Brad and Neale) believe that staying out of the past and not projecting into the future, but rather, staying in our experience right here, right now, is the way to come to love the truth and the telling of it, and then to love ourselves, and finally, to love each other. We believe that Love and Truth are really the same thing, that the two go hand in hand, and that to the degree that we are not telling the truth, the whole truth, and nothing but the truth, we are not totally loving.

That we've done this in the past is understandable. Fear is a powerful thing. But it doesn't have to last forever, and it must not if we are ever going to change the way things are in our world and in our individual lives.

And that is what many people want to do. Because the way we are creating our lives now, collectively and individually, is not working, and we can see that. Conflict is increasing. It is becoming a way of life. We are hurting people and killing people now over even our smallest disagreements. We've got school shootings, road rage, domestic violence, skyrocketing divorce and suicide rates, and now terrorism and its aftermath—an out-of-control society, really—revealing that to us, showing us that, telling us that. And so we want to change our world and our lives. And this book contains an incredible tool with which we can do that.

Honesty.

3

When You Hurt Your Fanger

(A Combination of Fear and Anger)

When we talk about transparency, which is the model that we use and the way that we articulate this idea of honesty, we are talking about total transparency in our relationships. As we were writing this book, the two of us realized that we'd come to a point of disagreement on some aspects of this. This led to a series of back-and-forth comments between us as we sought to clarify our points of view. Ultimately we came to a place of reconciliation in our dialogue; then Brad said, "Hey, let's let everyone know that we disagree, and see how we used telling the truth to each other as a means of staying connected and moving forward. Let's put our disagreements in the book!"

So here it is. We share it in the hope that when you see how and where we ended up, having traveled down that path with us, you will know more than you did about moralism, anger and individual and social transformation.

NDW: Many people say, "Well, you know, there are times when you can't be transparent. There are times when transparency, when total honesty, turns into brutality." And that can be true, depending upon how the truth is delivered. I knew a teacher once who was called Futzu, which is a Chinese word loosely translated as "master." He was a martial arts teacher. He used to say, "Speak your truth, but soothe your words with peace."

BB: I don't agree with that and don't cotton to it a bit. Futzu wasn't saying anything different than the usual pablum. This ends up encouraging people to be tactful. I don't like tactfulness. It is usually just another form of lying. If he meant, "Be centered in peace, even if you cuss somebody out," that might work for me. But most people don't interpret it that way. Most Westerners hear that as a moral "should" and a quite damaging one. They hear it as "Say what you must but be careful to phrase it in such a way as to not offend anyone or hurt anyone's feelings."

Lots of Eastern teachers are not aware of the listening into which they are speaking—not aware that their words become empty morals, fitted into the previously existing meaning which our Judaic/Christian heritage has already built into us. The moral dictate to "soothe your words with peace" fits right into the disease of moralism of the culture you and I were raised in.

The truth hurts sometimes. I think we need to hurt each other with the truth and stick with each other until we get over it. It is not unbearable hurt and it is not the same as physical hurt, as in an injury.

What gets "injured" is the person's ego, or their view of themselves. Calling verbal attacks the same as physical attacks is a form of psychosis. When we make physical pain and emotional pain equivalent to each other we make a big mistake.

I do not think we should be careful not to hurt each other's feelings, and I think the lack of that distinction between literal physical pain and emotional upset is the source of the kind of dancing on eggshells bullshit and resultant fury from lying about judgments and emotional reactions that our culture oozes. Nothing depends on how the truth is delivered. We are not running a charm school here. Brutality has to be reserved for actual physical hurt. Honesty is not brutality.

NDW: I agree with you that "brutality" is the wrong word—too evocative, too strong a word—to use in describing the process of total truth telling. I agree that there is a huge difference between physical "brutality" and the kind of hurt that can come from hearing the truth from another. I take your point that the word "brutality" is overdrawn. But the word "cruelty" is not, and cruelty to the heart is no less an offense against who we are than brutality to the body. It hurts less physically, yes of course that is true. But it still hurts. While "brutality" may be a wrong word, the word "cruelty" may be very apt indeed—and mental cruelty is not acceptable between loving human beings in my world— not even in the service of honesty. Is intimacy at the cost of kindness the highest priority?

BB: Intimacy is indeed a high priority. And intimacy frequently comes after great unkindness.

NDW: My question was, is intimacy at the *cost* of kindness the *highest priority?* My question refers to choice—to the ultimate choices we make in human relationships. My awareness is that it is possible to be intimate and honest without having to be cruel or unkind, ever.

BB: I disagree. I am of the opinion that you were raised in a worse version of the charm school than I was, and your ever present concern for carefulness not to offend, I find offensive. I love what we have said before and what comes after this, but I do not agree with you on your thoughts about framing the truth according to some kind of standard of "kindness." And my answer to that question, even though it is a loaded question, is yes. Intimacy at the cost of kindness *is* the highest priority.

NDW: You're an exceptional human being, in my experience, and I think you have some anger in you (that you've been lied to a lot in your life?) and I think that it is deep seated and that it distorts the part of you that would never be knowingly cruel to anyone. What is cruelty? Is it cruel to tell the truth to someone in a hurtful way? Can't a hurtful truth be told in a way that is not cruel?

BB: I think there is a further distinction necessary. We agree that sometimes the truth hurts. But I do not agree that "cruelty" to the mind is the same as "cruelty" to the heart. Compassion is *ruthless* to the mind and *completely confirming* to the heart. e.e. cummings once said, " If a poet is anyone, he is someone who is abnormally fond of that precision which creates movement." As a therapist and group leader I consider myself to be an artist of that sort. I create movement when I offend the mind to rescue the being from the jail of the mind. I love the being of the person I am in contact with, and I am practiced in a certain, almost surgical precision, in *offending* the *mind* while *loving* the *being*.

To confuse compassion with kindness in confronting the beliefs of the mind—even when the person thinks that who they are is their mind—is a mistake many less effective therapists and counselors make. Some of the therapeutic interventions in my own personal life have been shocking and hurtful and very beneficial—roughly the equivalent of tearing off a Band-Aid, short hairs and all—though I ended up greatly appreciating the assistance given in that way.

Not only that—but many of the counselors and coaches I am in contact with, in training, often have a related kind of experience with people we see. We get mad at people we love for the way they are mistreating themselves with their own minds. People are much more cruel to themselves than we are. Exposing the ridiculousness of that self-cruelty is our job and it is often a painful experience for the person so exposed.

Many people take great pride in being severely self-judging and we know they are ego-driven idiots to do so. It is our job to tell them that. Attachment to a negative self-judgment is just as egotistical as to a positive one. They need to be told just that, by someone who loves them, however many times and however many ways it takes, in order to be assisted in freeing themselves from the jail of their own minds. Then the question becomes, "Should we love this person and hurt their feelings, or should we be 'kind' and leave them to their familiar self-torture?" Or, "Should we offend this person to the extent that they may walk out forever, or leave them alone in their uncomfortable and noisy little minds?"

When I am truly compassionate and in contact with another being, loving them and using my mind to interrupt their mind, I can say, with love, "You poor dumb bastard, you've got your head so far up your ass, you can't even reach your ear to pull it out!" And I find it is quite possible to be completely bonded with that *being* and communicate at the same time my complete love and acceptance of the "Being Who Notices"— which is that human being's fundamental identity, just as it is mine. I offend the mind. But I actually *honor* the *being* by telling them that their *mind* is as full of shit as a Christmas turkey. I can, and do, do this. Most of the time such a confrontation ends in laughter and tears of gratitude and liberation for both of us.

You were very nice about it, but you just honored me by telling me that you loved me and that you think I have unresolved feelings about anger. You were kind and I got it and it worked. I just loved you and told you, basically, how in my opinion you were full of shit. And come to think of it, I was fairly nice about it too. We're probably both right. These statements could be interpreted as cruel or hurtful but, in fact, they made me feel closer to you, and I believe, you to me. Neither one of us got hurt or offended much, even though our minds might have taken the opportunity to do so, if they wanted to.

But to take a moral stand about always being kind has the same pitfalls as any other moral stand of the mind, and it reinforces one of our central cultural sicknesses. That's why I say moralism is the opposite of compassion. Moralism about compassion is the worst of all.

NDW: This is not about "moralism," it is about spirituality. And the two are not the same in my world. "Kindness" is a spiritual quality, not a moral issue. In my reality gentleness, softness, and kindness are states of being, not moral imperatives. May I give you an example? I would never use the language that you use to make the points that you make. I do not believe such language is necessary to make those points. Not even to make them with impact. Indeed, I observe that it *reduces* the impact of your points to use such language.

I do not believe that it is necessary to talk like Howard Stern. I would rather talk like Mahatma Gandhi. I observe that abrasiveness rankles and gentleness heals.

BB: Sometimes rankling heals too. According to Erik Erikson's biography on him, Gandhi was pretty damn mean to his wife and kids.

NDW: Oh, my God, I hope we're not going to be judging me in some future year based on some writer's idea about me! Ha!

BB: Erik Erikson is not just some writer. He is one of the greatest minds of the Twentieth Century, and he knew that the devil was in the details. But, of course, you will be judged in some future year based on some writer's idea about you, as will we all, and there is not much we can do about it!

NDW: Brad, my point here is that it is possible to tell someone that you believe they are hurting themselves and others with their mind without hurting them with your mind. Do you agree?

BB: It's possible. In fact I would even say that most of the time it's possible, and when it can be done it is fine to do. It's also possible to tell them and hurt them and stay with them until they get over it. When we get mad, we have to experience it and get over it. When we get hurt, we have to experience it and get over it. When we get mad and hurt each other we have to stick with our experience and stick with each other until we get over it. It happens. It is not a bad thing. It is a good thing. Greater intimacy occurs. Forgiveness occurs. A new and greater bonding and trust occurs. I appreciate the other person for hanging in there with me, and they appreciate me for the same. We go on. We forgive each other and go on.

NDW: Well, my friend, when you say, "When we get mad, we have to experience it and get over it. When we get hurt, we have to experience it and get over it. When we get mad and hurt each other we have to stick with our experience and stick with each other until we get over it," I agree with you, of course. I have said those same things many times. What I am discussing here, however, is the part *that we play* in the other person's experience of hurt by the way in which we deliver our truth. I am saying, over and over again here, that it is always possible to find a kind way to say your truth, and that words like "asshole" and "full of shit" and "sonofabitch" are not necessary, nor are they even productive. That is what I am saying, Brad. I am saying, "Speak your truth, but soothe your words with peace."

Of course anger happens, Brad. Of course, people allow themselves to feel hurt. Yes, these things happen. And yes, I agree with you that a new and greater bonding and trust occurs after we forgive each other. I agree with all of that. Where I do not feel in harmony with you is in the area of what I am going to call "Message Delivery." You seem to be saying to me that it is okay, it is all right, to speak to someone in the most abusive language, so long as that language represents your truth. I do not find that this works for me. This approach to truth-telling would not speak to me of who I am, nor who I choose to be.

You say, Brad, that in your opinion this is because I was "raised in a worse version of the charm school" than you were. Yet it is your approach, my friend, which feels to me to be very much a reflection of the "school of life" in which most people were raised, in which we believe that "nice guys finish last," and that any measure, including violence—and emotional and mental cruelty is violence—is justified to solve the most difficult problems.

BB: Here we go again. Mental cruelty is not violence. It is hurting the person's feelings, and it can be quite hurtful, but it is not violence. It hurts the person's feelings because of the person's attachment to their image of who they are or how things should be. This is why, many times, nice guys *do* finish last.

NDW: Gosh, Brad, we really do have a major, major difference of opinion here. And, apparently, a difference in life experience. I am *very* clear that mental cruelty is violence, and it is violence of the first rank. People are not their bodies, Brad. People are their souls. They are spirits *with* a body, but they are not bodies. When the Bad Guys capture the Good Guys and want to truly break a person—keep him alive, but break him—they do not try to beat him to a pulp, because with the really strong, that just won't work. They just wind up killing him and not get-ting out of him anything they wanted to get out of him. What they do is try to break his spirit. Every interrogator knows this.

Hard labor—physically painful—is not the harshest punishment. Solitary confinement is. "Mental cruelty is not violence?" Whoa. I beg to differ with you, my friend. And, in my world, knowingly being abrasive, abusive, and unkind in the delivery of one's truth is cruel, and, therefore, a form of violence.

Brad, I like your approach to life in terms of your encouraging people to always tell the truth, and I admire your own practice of always telling the truth to your family, friends and clients. I think we've pretty well established here that we both agree on that approach to life. I simply do not agree with your idea that it is okay to say your truth hurtfully. If you do this in therapy, as you say you do, that would feel to me like using the energy that created a problem to solve the problem.

BB: So what's wrong with that?

NDW: Einstein says that this is a form of insanity. Insanity, he says, is using the same energy that created a problem to try to solve it.

BB: No, he said, you can't solve a problem from the same perspec-tive in which it occurred. That is, with regard to perspective, insanity was to do the same thing over and over again expecting a different result.

NDW: Like killing people in order to stop people from killing people. Or using violence to stop people from using violence, such as the parent who hits his son, screaming, "How many times do I have to tell you to stop *hitting* your *little brother?*"

BB: I resent you for that analogy and I think it is unfair and doesn't fit. (So this means I'm attached to an ideal about goodness, of appropri-ate analogies and an ideal about fairness, and my feeling response is resentment. Although typing the expression isn't as helpful in getting over it as telling you in person, it helps a little). Also, I don't like the expression "your truth." I do not believe that there is "your truth" and "my truth" simply because opinions are not the truth. The truth is the truth of *experience.* Telling the truth is reporting what you *notice,* whether it is a sensation, a thought you have, or something you have done or observed in the world. The truth, which is the basically the same for everyone is the *truth of experience.* It's a report of what you *notice.* You can tell the truth *that you have an opinion* and say what it is, but the only honesty involved is that it is a reporting of the thoughts you notice at the time.

I acknowledge that what you notice may be different from what I notice. But what I *think* about what I notice and what you *think* about what you notice are basically bullshit, but we need to report it for the sake of honesty and for mutual self-correction.

Truthfulness is what sets you free. Truthfulness is reporting what you notice. *It includes saying what you don't think you should say at times.* It means following *feeling* rather than ideals. As e.e. cummings said, "(One) who worries about the syntax of things will never wholly kiss you." And following feeling and experiencing it and reporting honestly both feelings and opinions is what allows you to feel your way through things, and get over attachment to opinions, and change them. It is a little scary to follow feeling because you don't have as much presumed certainty as you do when you think you know what you should do. But as it turns out, less illusion of control equals more freedom.

NDW: In your case, you say that you hurt people in order to stop people from hurting people—including themselves. I believe that hearing the words you speak, being called the names you use, hurts people. Especially if those words are coming from someone they respect.

I believe that you think such shock talk is sometimes necessary to wake people up. I do not. In my world, a verbal slap in the face is not required, nor is it nearly as effective as a verbal hug. It is not about the hug being morally right. It is about the hug being more effective. More healing. And, for me, more of a spiritual statement of love, and of Who I Am.

BB: Well, we may not be too far apart here in actuality. Somehow people do get that I love them. Maybe it's because I have a Southern accent, or my paying attention to them so carefully is clear, or that they can tell that I have heard them. They get that I am on their side. And I am. And when they give themselves permission to hear me and to react—including cussing me back—I love it. Then it is not me being the authority who is telling them how to live, but another human being trying to work things out just like them. I don't do it just to shock. I do it to get through the usual defenses of the mind. Maybe it's a Southern thing. Although my friend Raven, who grew up in New York says, "It's a New York thing."

NDW: For me, every act is an act of self-definition. I do not choose to define myself as a person who compares another human being to an asshole, or who calls someone a sonofabitch. Not even in the name of "tough love." *Especially* not in the name of *any* kind of love.

BB: We are close to agreement here and yet still far apart. We agree that who you are and who I am are beings in love. In our essence, we are both beings who notice. But when we get to the choice part, or the self-definition part, or the part where we are performing or behaving to define who we are socially, we start to part ways. You are middle-class Catholic. I am white trash heathen. We have both been lucky enough to discover love. We manifest it in somewhat different ways.

Here is what I believe, at least for today. We are beings. We have minds. Our minds make judgments and compare, self-judge and judge others. We get mad because of attachment to being right about all these judgments. We either tell the truth about the judgments and go ahead and be mad when we are mad, or we don't. I am sure you agree that if we "act nice" when we feel mad, and we're "acting nice" because we have some kind of spiritual ideal, it is a lie. And it is very poisonous to other people, particularly with children, but with anyone at any time, to play nice when you don't feel nice. Our disagreement is at that point of self-definition (or rather social-self definition), because who you are, we have already agreed, is a being who notices in the moment, or a being who creates the world in the moment, whom we (might) call Presence, or God.

When you are manifesting behavior, through choice, defining who you are to yourself and in the eyes of other people, it is one of the places where you have to be meticulous about telling the truth. If you "act nice" to preserve your image or because of some spiritual ideal, you are lying and poisoning nevertheless. This is commonplace. This the source of a lot of the built up fury I see in a lot of people, particularly with couples. I think it is better to point out this particular kind of hypocrisy than to be in danger of catering to it. I don't doubt that your kindness is authentic, or that you value kindness, or that you choose to be kind. I believe you have a blind spot when you project a kind of even temperedness onto others.

NDW: Well, Brad, I don't think that we are going to see eye-to-eye on this, and that is okay. I do not share your reality that if I "act nice" when I am feeling mad, and I'm acting nice out of "some kind of spiritual idea," that it is a lie. Quite to the contrary, I think that it is the grandest truth of Who I Really Am. I very often *do* act nice even though I'm feeling mad. And can you believe this next statement? I think it is possible for *everyone* to "feel mad, nicely." I do not experience that this sort of behavior is "poisonous" to others.

Anger and violence are not intrinsically linked; anger and hurtfulness are not irrevocably married; anger and abrasiveness do not have to go hand in hand; and anger and verbal abuse are not essential or inevitable partners.

BB: No they are not, and I have not said so. But sometimes they are partners and *you live a lie when you monitor yourself by withholding, NOT speaking your judgments, or honestly expressing how you feel.*

NDW: In my cosmology, anger is one of five natural emotions (grief, anger, fear, envy, love). It is quite natural to become angry, and anger is not something that we should ever sublimate or hide, "sit on" or deny. On this we agree. We both believe that anger should be truthfully expressed. When you're mad, say you're mad. When you're upset, say you're upset. But you can say it nicely. You do not have to, but you can. And in my heart and in my soul and in my mind I cannot find a reason in the world not to.

I do not find it necessary, useful, effective or advisable—if peace, trust, and greater intimacy are the objectives—to announce or share one's anger with abrasiveness, verbal abuse or name-calling.

The expression of anger in order to resolve anger is the longest way to peace. It feels to me, as well, to be a very primitive way.

BB: I certainly hope it is primitive. The civilized way sure as hell doesn't work.

4

Idealism, Anger and Kindness

NDW: You have said, Brad, "If you 'act nice' to preserve your image or because of some spiritual ideal, you are lying and poisoning nevertheless." I don't know about preserving an image, Brad, because when you say *image* it feels as if you are talking about an idea about oneself as opposed to the reality of oneself—or, as we might say, one's experienced self.

BB: Yes. Precisely. That is what I wish to distinguish. There is a difference between one's idea of oneself and one's experienced self.

NDW: That may very well be what an image of oneself is, but an "ideal" is another matter altogether. I think an ideal is something one works towards, and I think that is worthy work. Perhaps we ought not seek to preserve an image of ourselves, but I hope that we will always seek to preserve an ideal about ourselves. We work in this world to preserve ideals all the time. And in my own life, I seek to create an ideal self every day—ideal according to my own measurements and definitions, not someone else's. "Conversations with God" calls this "the next grandest version of the greatest vision ever you held about Who You Are," and that is what I seek to create and experience in and through and with my life.

BB: Well, I think that is a kind of old-fashioned way to think about it. I think that idealism is *itself* the sickness, *any* idealism, regardless of the value idealized. I think idealism is the essential thing one must cure in order to use the mind rather than be used by it. I think that detachment from ideals, rather than attachment to ideals, allows one to use values rather than be used by them. I think we get attached to ideals easily and that it is the source of most of our problems. For example, an attachment to an ideal about always being nice when you are angry could be the source of a lot more anger.

NDW: My ideal is that honesty and kindness go hand in hand. Indeed, in my world, honesty IS kindness. I think that you agree with this.

BB: Yes, I do. But at the times I am not attached to it as an ideal I find that I am able to be more powerful and loving as a result. Honesty is sometimes interpreted as cruelty, and I don't intend to be controlled by another person's interpretation. Otherwise why even bother to talk? The very heart of superficiality and isolation is to figure out what people want to hear and then say that. What is vital is the *quality of contact* between the two beings and honesty is what allows that to be. Whether it fits the mold of an apparent ideal or not is entirely secondary.

NDW: And I agree that we cannot spend our lives protecting someone, or others, from the feelings they allow to come up for them in the face of hearing the truth. I do not agree that we should ignore kindness altogether.

BB: Nor do I assert that . . .

NDW: In my world, it is no less cruel to hit someone in the heart with attacking words than it is to hit someone in the chest with attacking fists. I find great truth in the teaching, "Speak your truth, but soothe your words with peace."

There is a place for compassion in the human experience, and it extends beyond physical compassion to psychological compassion.

BB: Well, of course it does. I don't think that honesty and kindness can-**not** go hand in hand, and never have I said that. They can go hand in hand. *We must not, however make it a standard of conduct to override honesty.* There is plenty of advocacy in the culture we grew up in to use kindness as a rationalization for withholding the truth—"if you can't say something nice, don't say anything at all."

Being tactful, being "politically correct," or being polite is constantly taught in school and at home as primary values. I have gotten to know intimately several generations of people who were suffering from the lying that those moral "shoulds" are the source of. This suffering is much greater than the pain caused by telling the truth to another person about your judgments of him or her, and hurting their feelings.

Furthermore, *being angry* rather than telling some story about how you are mad, makes all the difference in the world about whether you can get over it or not. The story is an ego performance, done to live up to your image of yourself, or your ideal about how you should behave. It is not who you are, it is still a performance. Sometimes angry words or triggered reactions hurt, but you can get beyond it, and often do, if you commit to hanging in there to feel your way through to forgiveness with each other. Getting over things is through *telling the truth and feeling your way through,* not thinking your way around. An agreement to do this, though at times hard to keep, is one that works much better than an agreement to try to be nice and careful not to hurt each other's feel-ings. Constant lying for the sake of kindness hurts in a way that is very hard to recover from, and does ongoing damage to the person until the truth gets told.

When you are in contact, being to being, with another person, what is honest is to *have your reactions and stay in contact.* When you moni-tor your reactions according to an ideal, you are abandoning contact with the person in order to control your performance. You remove your attention from the being you are in contact with, pay attention to your own mind and your own performance, for the sake of your pre-existing spiritual ideal, and in that moment you are no longer in contact with the person. This breaking of contact is not only unnecessary but it makes it more likely that you have begun talking to someone else in your mind rather than the person you are talking to right in front of you, while still pretending to talk to that person in front of you. So you end up talking to your own imagination in front of you.

I am not just talking about counseling situations here, where you are somewhat protected from being offended by your role as an authority, but real situations with people you live and work with. If, in fact, there is any actual moral obligation here, it is to go against the cultural flow, where we have been taught that who we are *is* our performance, which is the source of so many people living a lie. We've been taught that we are our grades, how much money we make, what other people think of us . . . I purposely teach people to resist that, not go along with it. Love and forgiveness occur outside the bounds of such control, not because of it.

NDW: Listening to your comments, Brad, it feels that I have not been clear on what I believe about kindness and truth. I do not believe that kindness should "override" honesty. I believe that it should go *with* honesty.

If you see yourself, if you wish to experience yourself and choose to create yourself, as Honesty and Kindness, it should never be necessary to step away from one in order to step into the other. The two are not, and never have to be, mutually exclusive. And I use the word never advisedly.

"Soothe your words with peace" does not mean replace your truth with lies, it means speak your truth with kindness. I believe that there are always ways to do that. I do not believe that kindness has no role to play in the conduct of human affairs and that honesty justifies cruelty. I want to repeat that. I do not believe that honesty justifies cruelty.

BB: And I want to repeat that that is too simplistic a formulation to fit the complexity of compassion. IF YOU FEEL ANGRY AND YOU SPEAK KINDLY IT'S A LIE. Of course, there is a place for kindness. I love and am kind to many people, and they are to me. In our community of friends at Radical Honesty Enterprises we love each other and we sometimes have knock-down drag-out fights. But we end up having such a love fest before the day is over we can hardly stand it. This is the heart of what I want to share with the world. Tell the truth about your self-righteousness and get over it. We all have this disease of moralism. We can cure it by being honest about what we feel. We can't do anything at all about it by putting on some act about it because we want to be "spiritual."

The possibility of true compassion goes way beyond simplistic rules of order about political correctness. Love can only exist if the truth be told. Love cannot exist if the truth not be told. If hurt occurs in the course of the truth being told, then let it occur and feel your way through it; the other side is liberation. People can get over having their feelings hurt. People can get over being offended. What they can't get over is lying and being lied to.

The main rationalization for lying in our whole culture is "I didn't want to hurt anyone's feelings." The second major rationalization for lying is "I didn't want to offend anybody." I can't tell you how many times I have heard this argument in defense of lying.

I recommend that you hurt people's feelings and stay with them until you both get over it. I recommend that you offend people and stay with them until you both get over it. I recommend that you do the same when hurt or offended by others. Most "hurts," like most "offenses," are just bullshit anyway. You discover that by repeatedly having the experience of getting over them. After a while you see that *the benefit of forgiving others is your own liberation.*

NDW: Like you, Brad, I have personally counseled thousands of people, but I have found something different from what you say you have observed. You have said, "The main rationalization for lying in our whole culture is 'I didn't want to hurt anyone's feelings.' The second major rationalization for lying is 'I didn't want to offend anybody.' I can't tell you how many times I have heard this argument in defense of lying."

Well, I have heard that too, of course. But when I have heard it, I have questioned it. I have said, "My friend, I want to invite you to reexamine what you have just said to me. You have just said that you have not told the truth because you did not want to offend, or because you did not want to hurt someone's feelings. I understand that by not telling the truth you believe that you are protecting someone else. Yet in my own life I observe that when I am not telling the truth, more often than not it is me that I am protecting. Might this be possible with you as well? What do you think?"

Of course, they nearly always acknowledge, when hearing this, that this is exactly what is going on. Then I say to them, "Thank you for seeing that. Now if there was a way to share your truth with another without being hurtful in the delivery of it, what do you think it would be?"

And do you know what? They almost always come up with a way to do that.

BB: Well, I like that just fine. I think it is a good and helpful intervention.

NDW: Now, mind you, I make a point of discussing how the truth is *delivered,* not how it might be *received.* Even when we are kind, another person may choose to *feel* hurt. That is what is so. We cannot be responsible for that, *and we should not try* to be. If we try to be, *that* is when we become dysfunctional. I believe that this is what you are trying to say, Brad. This is what I hear you saying—that we ought not make ourselves responsible for how others choose to feel. We can only be responsible for ourselves.

Yet it seems to me that by speaking to others as you do, you are throwing the baby out with the bath water. You seem to be saying, "Since I am not responsible for your reactions to me, and since your feelings are your own, and since I believe that you will get over them in any event if I just stay here in the room with you, I can say anything I want to you, in whatever way that I want, and do it with impunity." I think that you see this as the height of personal integrity, and that's interesting. I would see it as abandonment of my integrity—of my very sense of Who I Am—to speak to another as you do.

BB: No. I don't think people choose what they feel. People react and call it a choice but it really isn't. It's a rationalization of a feeling reaction, so that they can play like they were in control when they weren't. And I *do* think I am responsible for people's reactions to me. I am responsible for the way my life goes and the source of what happens to me.

NDW: Brad, we are diverging more and more the longer we speak. So what I am finding is that we do not have to agree on all the fine points of human psychology for us to write a book together. But let me make clear here my own ideas about what you've just said.

Brad, in my workshops and seminars I teach exactly the opposite of what you've just said. I tell participants that the world says that "people cannot choose what they feel, that people react and call it a choice but it really isn't," and that "it's a rationalization of a feeling reaction, so that they can play like they were in control when they weren't." That's what the "experts" say, and people believe them.

BB: Yes, I am one of the "experts" who says that.

NDW: But what I know and experience in my world is that feelings *can* be chosen. We can *choose to feel a certain way* about a thing, and, moreover, we can *decide ahead of time* how we are going to feel when and if something in particular happens. This is not a "rationalization of a feeling reaction," this is a *masterful creation.*

Masters do this. And students on their way to mastery. This is called mastery in living. This is exactly what I share in my Recreating Yourself retreats, based on the "Conversations with God" material. It is transformative. It changes people's lives, moving them from being at the effect of their own experience to being *at cause in the matter.*

So I think that we have fundamental, a very fundamental, difference in how we see ourselves and all human beings, Brad.

BB: We do. I do *not* think that people choose what they feel. I do think that people react and call it a choice, but that it really isn't. Furthermore, I think we are one hundred percent responsible for creating how things work out with other people, but the interaction might have some rough patches to go through to get to resolution of our reactions to each other. If we stick to it, the communication reaches clarity and completion. If we cop out we say, "Well, it's not my fault how you react." That is just placing blame. I am not talking about blame now, but about responsibility.

People who are Masters don't get angry *precisely because they are not attached to ideals having to do with control.* They had to observe and tell the truth rather than monitor their reactions in order to get to that place of mastery. Although I do agree with you that what is transformative for people is to grow beyond being victims to *being at cause in the matter.* It is just that the way you get there *is not through idealism of any kind.* Idealism is kind of a stage of development to be grown beyond. That is done through telling the truth about what you notice, including what you notice you are attached to and what you feel. It is through sharing honestly with others, and hearing what they have to share, that you surrender the illusion of control that having ideals provides. You then discover the possibility of actual control through ongoing re-discovery of experience and sharing.

NDW: I like the way this brings up the question of what place kindness has in the human experience—real kindness and false kindness. Is real kindness the failure to express what others may choose to experience as hurtful? No. I think we do both agree on this, do we not? We are disagreeing, I think, on how that truth is best delivered. But I think we both agree that hiding the truth is an unkindness.

BB: Yes. But let me say again, just one more time for emphasis. Kindness as a moral principle, imposed as a "should" by the mind, is the cause of a great deal of repression and anger. So if you talk about kindness, you have to talk about two kinds of kindness. There is kindness as a *feeling response* to another person. There is kindness as a *moral imperative.* I think that the place in which you impose the moral "should" makes you a phony, being "kind" because you think you "should." If kindness occurs at a particular place and time you are authentic, and if it occurs at another place and time it can be inauthentic. Take the golden rule, "Love others as you love yourself."

NDW: Do unto others as you would have it done unto you.

BB: Yes. Now you *will do that automatically,* as an affirmation, *out of your contact with the Holy Human Prototype of another being,* because you see that you and the other are the same, so you treat yourself and them the same way. Out of your *experience* you'll do that. But if you turn this into a Moral Principle, you could end up with something like the Crusades, because you'll insist on a certain kind of behavior, and you'll end up killing people if they aren't the "right kind of person" doing the "right kinds of things."

So to me this is a critical issue. It's not something you can easily resolve by having an insight or treating it as a problem to be solved. What I know is that honesty must precede the imposition of moral rules. You are honest for the sake of your own freedom and to ensure the quality of the contact with another person. If you are able to remain in touch with that person, being to being, you will constantly be operating from the golden rule. If you try to be honest because it's a moral dictate, you'll end up with something like the Crusades. Honesty in contact also includes anger. So there's no way to not acknowledge anger. We have to experience it and go through it honestly, or else it becomes stored in angry righteousness, or suppressed for the sake of obedience to a moral dictate.

NDW: I'm missing the connection. I agree with you fundamentally. My mind is saying, "Wait a minute, let me see if I can follow this." Help me understand. Why would following honesty as a moral dictate because you've been told to be honest lead to something like the Crusades? I can't make the connection.

BB: I've seen lots of people recovering from Catholic Parochial School in therapy over the course of twenty-five years as a psychotherapist in Washington, D.C. What those nuns were teaching those children (in a disciplined and systematically kind of hateful way, often, as I've heard told in lots of life stories, with a morally righteous form of instruction) was how to be phony. They were teaching them to have their real life in secret and on the side, and always play like they were "good little boys" and "good little girls" for their public presentation of who they were. They were taught to do this at any cost. So, as you grow up it becomes,

"I'm going to try to play like I'm a good man. I'm going to try to play like I'm a kind person. I will always present an image of kindness and goodness wherever I go. Whether I get mad or not, I'll just suppress it and try to be 'good.'"

NDW: I see that model, but how does that lead to the Crusades?

BB: Well, the kind of anger that gets built up behind that lying must find an outlet . . .

NDW: . . . And ultimately explode.

BB: Yes. Ultimately it's going to come out as a conflict with another individual, or it's going to be a war. If you can get enough people on your side who are in alignment with your method of repression, who are convinced that those other people over there are the problem, you have a war.

NDW: Yes, because after all, we are so nice over here, we are doing it so right, we are making the right choices, and you know we really do love you people over there, but you're not making the right choices.

BB: So we're going to kill you!

NDW: Well, I can follow that. More than one person has died at that crossroads.

BB: I would have thought that if this last century (the bloodiest of all) has taught us one valuable thing, it would have something to do with the relativity of values themselves, and the relativity of the imposition of values. You can't simply impose values on yourself and other people through force. You can't make yourself and other people adopt them. Everyone will do the opposite no matter what. It's the imposition of that moralism that *is* the problem, and we are starting out the new century not having learned a thing.

NDW: What I have been saying all along here is that kindness is not a moral issue with me, it is a spiritual one. It is a definition of Who I Am, not a statement about How I Must Be. Since receiving and writing "Conversations with God" I have taught that there are no absolutes and that morality cannot be legislated or imposed, but must come authentically from one's sense of self.

BB: Yes, I like all that. And I profoundly agree.

NDW: I wonder whether the human race will ever learn that.

BB: If we keep sharing honestly and they keep buying our books they will!

NDW: I can't argue with that!

Here our dialogue about this ended, and as a conclusion to these last two chapters—which we hope served the dual purpose of modeling how truth-telling works, and making some important points for you to ponder—we both agreed to share the following words with you, which we have shared with each other:

> *I honor the place within you where*
> *the entire universe resides.*
> *I honor the place within you of love and light,*
> *of peace and truth.*
> *I honor the place within you where,*
> *when you are in that place in you*
> *and I am in that place in me,*
> *there is only one of us.*
> *Namasté.*

5

What Are the Most

Honest Moments?

onest moments are moments in which truth is available to us, immediately and clearly. These are always what Neale calls in his latest book, "Moments of Grace." These moments can be created for us by another person, or by a circumstance or situation that reveals a great truth to us.

In the most radical moments of honesty in our lives we often cry. That does not mean we are sad. More often, in fact, it means we are relieved, or joyful, or both. Brad likes to give as an example what he considers to be one of the most impactful moments of honesty he says he's experienced in his life. It was when his children were born.

BB: I was there for the deliveries of several of my children. I have five children. I was there for the births of four of them. There's something about that experience of being so into the act of creation itself and participating with the woman who's bearing my child that causes me to drop my mind's interpretation and connects me with noticing. When I'm so fully present, I'm usually overwhelmed by feeling, and then, if I don't run away from it, I cry. Usually, I cry. And, on the other side of that crying, I'm still in contact and still in feeling, but I don't feel so overwhelmed with it. We've all been taught to hold our breath when we start feeling something.

NDW: Literally. Not just figuratively, but literally. I tell people in my workshops, "Breathe, just keep breathing." They want to stop breathing.

BB: Right. (Laughing) It's supposed to be a function of the involuntary nervous system, but most of us have imposed upon it our voluntary nervous system, so we are using striated muscle tissue to keep smooth muscle tissue from working in order to make sure we don't feel too much. It's that fear of feeling too much that we keep coming back to in this conversation.

NDW: Yet "Conversations with God" says that feelings are the language of the soul. So if you want to get in touch with your soul, if you want to know what's true for you at the innermost part of your being, you cannot do so by segregating yourself from your feelings. You cannot do so by ignoring your feelings, or withholding your feelings, or condemning your feelings, or by being a good little boy or girl and pretending that they are not your feelings.

Releasing the love which is the soul is only possible through the expression of feelings. For when you express feelings, you express the soul, which is Love embodied in you. Love is the deepest feeling. It is at the bottom of it all. But to release it, you have to get everything else out. This includes the feelings that you may have that you may feel are not worthy of who you are, or want to be. If you repress those feelings, as we have noted earlier, you wind up becoming not loving, but dangerous.

•••

Expressing our true feelings requires one single and simple tool. Honesty.

Are There Situations in Which People Should Lie?

"But," some people ask, "aren't there some situations, some circumstances, in which telling the truth is simply not a good idea? Surely there must be some exceptions."

•••

NDW: I'm going to make a very radical statement here. I'm going to say that there is no time and no place in human affairs that not telling the truth is appropriate. Now, I've had cause to question that in recent years as audience members have come to me and said, "Well, you're a soldier behind enemy lines and 1600 of your fellow men are out there and the enemy is telling you to report their position and what their plans are. Wouldn't you lie then?" The answer I've given them is that I wouldn't lie, I'd tell the truth. The truth is: "I have no intention of telling you that."

This is very much like the Fifth Amendment, our own self-incrimination clause in this country. In the United States, citizens are not required to answer any question that they think could get them in trouble— because of the truth, or because *of how the truth might look.* When witnesses at Congressional hearings or before grand juries "take the Fifth," they simply say, "I refuse to answer the question on the grounds that it may tend to incriminate me." They are not lying. They are telling the absolute truth.

BB: Well, they are telling the truth that they are not going to tell the truth. I agree. Special provision has been made for situations of war and political intrigue, and for reasonable cause, given the context in which it occurs.

But taking the Fifth Amendment in personal relationships is different. You are not dealing with a battlefield situation or with the current version of the insane law of the land and its enforcers. You are dealing with a person who you know and with whom you have pledged to share the way your life is. Anything other than a temporary withholding is a lie in my book. (For instance, in the case of an emerging crisis, or you have an immediate deadline, or there's a child present whom you don't want to scare by yelling—the completion can be delayed briefly until an appointed time agreed upon by both.) But I think taking the Fifth Amendment in personal relationships is lying. Withholding is lying. It doesn't matter if you admit you are withholding you are still lying. It is bullshit to say you are withholding but not lying. My definition of lying includes withholding and I think people who have agreed to be in an intimate relationship, if they really want intimacy, have to agree that taking the Fifth Amendment is not one of their agreements. Quite the opposite. Taking the Fifth in personal relationships is a coward's way out.

However, I don't recommend that you tell the truth all the time.

NDW: You don't? Now, I'm surprised by that! I think, "Why, you liar you!" (Laughter) Well, when do you think that it's okay to lie, Brad?

BB: I have had lots of discussions about this. If you had Anne Frank in your attic and a Nazi knocks on the door and asks, "Are there any Jews in this house?"—Lie! I recommend that you lie.

And with other institutional representatives and authorities, when they're armed and you're in situations like that, use common sense. There's no reason for jeopardizing your life and the lives of other people if there's an insane person trying to make you do something who has the force of arms to back them. Go ahead and lie to them until you can overpower them or escape.

I was in the civil rights movement from 1959–64. I got shot at, bombed with a lead pipe bomb, beat up, arrested, detained and various other things. I was also in the anti-Vietnam War movement for seven years, and got arrested and beat up a couple of times there. During those years I read lots of reports about activities I was a part of, yet when I read them in "Time" magazine, I couldn't tell where the reporters had been—they weren't at the same place I was. Those stories were written by a committee and were all a bunch of interpretations with no description. Reports about what things *mean* are not the same as descriptions of what occurred. Lying is done so easily by the mind. All you have to do is leave some things out of a partial description and play up other aspects of a situation that occurred and give opinions about it.

I've got plenty of fury in me about authority anyway, as you rightfully perceive and anybody who reads my books can tell (laughing), and I'm glad that I do. By the time so-called reporters or committees of reporters give all of their interpretations of the meaning of what is going on, instead of saying what happened, their report is a lie. Most institutions lie to us in this way. So I lie right back to institutions occasionally, particularly if they can hurt me or people I care about.

For example, I occasionally lie to the FBI. Sometimes people with high security clearances come to see me in psychotherapy. Then, in order to keep their high security clearance current, the FBI comes to me with a signed form by the person who's been my client saying I can tell them everything the client has said in psychotherapy. (This revelation of how security clearances happen will certainly renew people's faith in Washington!)

The FBI agent says to me, "To your knowledge, has this person ever used illegal drugs?" I know very well that they have, and I say, "Not to my knowledge." I lie to them. I lie to them on purpose. I even enjoy it. Once I asked the FBI agent; "How about you? Have you ever smoked marijuana?" He said, "No." I said, "Okay, we're even now. Come on with your next bullshit question."

If you're in the criminal justice system in the United States of America for anything serious, you are a fool if you don't lie, because the system is set up expecting you to, and can only work if you do. People hire lawyers so that they can lie better. That's what lawyers are for. The criminal justice system is set up in order to *maintain* the lie that justice will emerge from whoever can argue the best to sell a *moralistic interpretation* of what happened as more important than a *full revelation and understanding* of what happened.

Usually when you're caught up in the criminal justice system you get a lawyer in order for him to distort the interpretations of what occurred, in such a way that you can win. That's what the whole system is set up for.

NDW: You're hitting something that I've said publicly when I discussed Bill Clinton's actions initially in the Monica Lewinski case. I didn't say that he did the right thing, I said I understand why he did what he did. People said, "How can you say you understand why he did that? He's the President. How can you, of all people, who are supposed to have this elevated sense of spirituality, say that you understand how a man can do that?"

I said, "Now wait a minute, you have to understand first of all that our entire society is constructed in such a way that it supports the Big Lie. It expected the President to lie about Lewinski and supported the Big lie." I'm sure that most of the people understood, when he first said what he said, that he wasn't telling the truth. He wasn't kidding anybody, but he lied because we punish people in this society for telling the truth.

BB: Absolutely.

NDW: He knew that he, and Lewinski, and the presidency itself, would have been punished, damaged, had he told the truth. The only mistake that Bill Clinton made was, he should have looked right at the camera and said; "You know, ladies and gentlemen, when I'm asked that question, here's the answer I want to give you. If you, the American people, if human society, would make it beneficial, profitable or even okay at some level for the truth to be told in all matters about government, personal lives, or anything, then you would probably get the truth a lot more of the time. When you make a person pay for the truth, sometimes with their very lives, or all that matters in their lives (even the life of this country and the presidency in this case), when you make the price of truth so high that to lie is the only alternative, then you get what you ask for. And you are not asking for the truth. You are asking for revenge."

BB: I agree with your interpretation, though I would have recommended that he be more radical. From the time that he adopted the "Don't ask, don't tell" policy for gays in the military, I gave up on Bill Clinton about being a man of courage. He's not a man of courage, he's a man of adaptation. Bill Clinton wouldn't ever have gone so far as to say what you said. That would have been too radical for him. But I'd go even further. I think he should have had a "fireside chat" with the whole nation, with Hillary and Chelsea and say, Jesse Jackson as moderator—and have everyone in the room tell about their sexual experiences in detail.

If I were Clinton I would have revealed all in detail. I would have said, "When Monica and I were in that room and had our cigar . . ." and I'd have told every detail of what happened and how much fun it was, and that I didn't do penetration sex because I felt guilty and that's what happened. Then he could say, "That is what I did. If you want to impeach me for that, it's up to you. Take it or leave it. The presidency is not that great of a job anyway." (Laughter)

NDW: That would have been the end of the discussion.

BB: Well, no, it wouldn't have. It would have been the beginning of a hell of a discussion, which I would have been happy to help with. He could have come out the greatest leader in the twentieth century. But he didn't have the stomach for it. He acted nice instead.

NDW: We could use some middle ground here. I wasn't saying that he shouldn't have been honest. I think the middle ground is, he could have said, "I did it." I understood why he lied, but if I had been Bill Clinton, I wouldn't probably have been as graphic as you, because I'm not sure that that level of graphic revelation is required by honesty. I think you and I do have a difference of opinion. I don't think honesty requires that.

If I had been Bill Clinton I think I would have said, "You know, I had sexual experiences with Monica Lewinski." I would have gone this far, I would have said, "I did not go to the ultimate level of sexual intimacy because I felt it was inappropriate to this flirtatious momentary experience I was having. I felt in my own value system that would have been a violation of my sacred trust with my wife, but a dalliance, touching now and then and other sexual intimacies, I admit it. I had that experience and that's what happened."

BB: That's pretty close, but no cigar. (Laughter) I still feel the details makes it easier on you because they're going to be going after all the details forever from that sort of teaser, so you might as well be right up front and just tell the whole truth. When you withhold a little like that they will pick at you until they get it all anyway.

I'm thinking someday about running for public office, and I'd like to run on a campaign of complete out-loud truth and say exactly where I've been and what I think and what I intend: "If I get elected I'm going to play golf most of the time and go on these little jaunts, only I'm not going to play like it's something for legitimate government business, I'm going to have a damn good time at your expense."

NDW: Warren Beatty's "Bullworth." Yeah, that was a great film. Can you imagine a politician who'll actually say it like it is?

BB: Not unless you or I do it! When Ralph Nader was nominated and entered the presidential race I went to the rally, and he came closer than most to being really honest.

6

Radical Honesty in Politics

The previous chapter really brings up the question: Is the American public ready for truth in politics? Is it ready for a candidate like Bullworth, someone who would just say it like it is and absolutely tell the truth? We don't know. But we'd like to think so. And we'd like to see a litmus test done. We'd like to see someone try it. Particularly after the 2000 presidential campaign, and the Florida fiasco, which was a mockery of everything that is truthful.

What happened in Minnesota is the closest to this litmus test that we've had. An honest man ran and an honest man got elected. Jesse Ventura. He speaks out loud, says what he thinks, what he feels. Even those who disagreed with him had to admire him for his honesty. He was saying, essentially, if you don't agree with me, for goodness sake don't vote for me. But how can you even know if you agree with me if I don't tell you what's true for me?

Since the 2000 election, there has been a lot of talk about reforming politics. All that our politicians have to do to reform politics is tell the truth about what they've done, what they think and what they feel. That's all. It's as simple as that. But it's hard to do if you're afraid to lose and if you'll do anything to win—including lie. Most politicians don't lie by commission. Some do, but not most. Most lie by omission. It is not what they say that is untruthful; it was what they fail to say that creates what they call "wiggle room" (read "untruth").

●●●

BB: If I were out there running for election, this would be my campaign: " I'm going to tell you the truth about what I think, about what I feel, about what I do, and about what I have done. My life's an open book. And I've done plenty of bad things—everybody has."

NDW: There's great freedom in that. I agree with you. I want to mention those three points again, because those three points really are important. They help to clarify what Radical Honesty is all about in practical terms. It is simply always telling the truth about what we've thought, what we've done, and how we feel. It really is as simple as that. I've learned that lesson in my life. In recent years when I've been interviewed, and I'm interviewed by everybody in the world, I just tell the truth.

"People" magazine" interviewed me and they wanted to know what my life was about and I just told them all the stuff that I've done. Everything. I told them, "You won't even have to do the research. Here are the telephone numbers, you can call them." The reporter was so disarmed by that. When it came out in "People" magazine, while they did say something about my having a "tangled past," they didn't go into nearly as much detail as they would have if that guy had spent three and a half weeks on the road digging up all the same stuff. He'd have to justify that, but I just laid it all out for him, and he thought, "Oh, so what" and just gave it a couple lines and there it was.

BB: You know, it seems like politicians would figure this out.

NDW: I thought, after Nixon blew it so badly with Watergate, that no other politician would ever again make the same mistake, and they've all made the same mistake ever since Clinton. Why can't they learn from something as obvious as the Nixon blunder? We are a strange species, aren't we, Brad? We don't learn. Not just about lying, but really about anything. I notice we are very slow on the uptake.

We're Just Not Learning From Our Own Experience

And why? Because we are not "experiencing our experience" most of the time. If we were experiencing our experience we would be learning, but we're living in the part of our minds that is *thinking,* not *noticing.* It is *interpreting,* not *observing.* It is believing past data, or projecting a future reality. We are living in our interpretations and projections; we are avoiding our actual experience. We don't even know what it is. We're trying to sell other people on the idea that our interpretation of our experience is what reality is, and they're trying to sell us on the idea that *their* interpretation of *their* experience is what reality is, while neither one of us is paying attention to what the reality *actually* is.

Werner Erhard had a lot to say about this in his "est Trainings," a personal growth program that was very popular early in the final quarter of the last century. He encouraged people to look at "what's so," instead of at their ideas of what's so based on past data or future projections.

Human beings do not often look at "what's so." A present experience is either dunked in messages from our past, thus it is "past-urized," or its focus is fuzzied by overlaid images from some imagined tomorrow, and thus it is "future-ized." This would be bad enough if the messages from our past were accurate ones, if they told us the truth. But most of the messages from our past (from which we draw our future projections) are messages given to us by other people, messages received from other sources—sources outside of ourselves whom we've assumed know all about life, all about what we are experiencing, and to whom we have thus turned over our authority.

But there is no authority and there is no truth except our own experience. Everything else is something that someone else is making up. That is why all true masters will never attempt to tell you What Is True. They will simply tell you what is True For Them. Then they will invite you to Your Own Experience. Anyone who claims to be a "master" and does not do this is not a master. Anyone who claims to be a teacher and does not do this is not a teacher. Anyone who claims to love you and does not do this does not love you. They merely love themselves—or their image of themselves—and wish to continue loving the image of themselves through you.

All of the above may not be true for you, but it is true in our experience. You will have to look to your own experience to see if it is true for you.

Teachers can lead you to your own experience, masters can guide you to your own experience, lovers can entice you to your own experience, but only you can have that experience. And only you can know what it is. You can tell others what it is, but they can't know what it is, experientially. No one can know that but you. We cannot ever have the same experience. Ever. We can have nearly the same experience, we can get close to the same experience, and we can call it the "same" experience, but it is not really the same, and it cannot be. Each of us is experiencing what we are experiencing through the filter of our own individuality.

Experiences are like snowflakes. There are no two alike. That is because we *are* the experience, and there are no two of US alike. In our universe, there is no separation between the Experience and The Experiencer. (In fact, there is no separation between anything at all—but that is another matter!)

The great political accidents and uproars of our time that are the most inspiring are those times in which teachers of this level of wisdom have gotten elected, or have gained power through non-violent protest. Gandhi, King, Havel, Tutu, Mandela and others who, because of a perspective that transcended the limitations of their social group, had a lot of trouble, but brought about a lot of growth that benefited a lot of people.

Be careful if you are one of those who might be tempted to think that this is all just "new age gobbledygook." Some pretty straight-laced scientists and quantum physicists have been saying for years now that "nothing which is observed is unaffected by the observer." In other words, we are creating our own reality. We are creating our own reality by being the experiencing organism. We are an organism that has sensations, and we have words that allow us to report reality in a descriptive way, through saying what we see, smell, hear etc. We are also in possession of a mind that distorts our report of our experience through interpretations based on records of past experience and cultural learning. When you think about this it's a wonder we communicate as well as we do!

Of course, this is exactly what has been said in Neale's five "With God" books, and Brad has made precisely the same point in "Radical Honesty," "Practicing Radical Honesty," "Radical Parenting," "The Truthtellers," "The Radical Honesty Rag" and other publications.

Does this mean that we cannot create a jointly-experienced reality? No. What it does mean is that our jointly-experienced reality will not be identical from person to person. It will not be experienced in exactly the same way by every one of the experiencers. Furthermore, it won't be interpreted the same way by the minds of the experiencers. Yet we can co-create a reality that is experienced in a very, very similar way by very, very many people. In fact, we are doing that every day. It is called "living by agreement."

We all agree that a certain thing is a certain way, and we agree not to argue about that. In this way we can make some sense of our collectively created reality, and we can pass on some previously agreed upon data and save each other a lot of time around that. The trick is to not get caught up in other people's agreements about too much of the really important stuff. That's the trick. The trick is to know when to step into The Illusion and when to step away from it. The trick is to know the difference between thoughts, which you think you are thinking but which are actually thinking you, and your experience of being alive in the here and now, as a being who notices.

"Communion with God" says that all of life is a collectively created illusion, and lists the Ten Illusions of Humans. This is a fascinating discourse and offers a new context within which to hold the entirety of our experience on this planet.

Barbara Marx Hubbard, the eminent thinker and futurist, says in her books "Conscious Evolution" and "Emergence" that we have moved into a place where we are now co-creating with greater and greater awareness the experiences that we are having, and, thus, who we are,

59

and what it means to be human.

Philosopher Jean Houston agrees. In her latest writing, "Jump Time," she asserts that the human race is moving into a period where more and more humans are creating a future on purpose, rather than a future that they more or less stumble into. Given our vastly improved technologies, all this is happening not a moment too soon. Yet even today most people are moving through the world unconsciously.

Werner Erhard urged us all to create consciously, with full awareness of what we are doing and why. And he said that the first step in that transformation of our lives was simply—here we go again!—telling the truth.

We echo that here. And one of the things we urge people to consciously create is a world without deception, without hidden agendas, without back door dealings, or under the table manipulations, or behind the scenes maneuverings, or out of sight agreements, or between the lines understandings, or *anything* that is not totally transparent. A world in which telling and living the truth carries the highest reward and is given the highest honor by society.

7

Intimacy Versus Managed Care

NDW: Still, Brad, you've talked about situations where you would lie, and I think I know what you're going to say here, but I want to return to the kind of question that I'm always asked at my lectures and workshops and public appearances.

Mom is dying; she's eighty-six, and the doctor goes into the other room and says to the kids, "She has a week." Do you go in and tell Mom, "You've got a week," so she can have a chance to get her affairs in order? She thinks it's not that serious. She knows she's ill, but she thinks, "I'm not at death's door yet." Now the doctor is in the next room telling you she's not going to make it through the week.

The question: Do you owe it to your mother to let her be responsible for her own reaction? Or do you think it's best to play God in that situation and just say, "What Mom doesn't know won't hurt her."? Then, when she realizes she's dying (if she is blessed at that moment to know what's going on), watch helplessly as she looks up at you with those last few breaths and says, "Excuse me, but you know, I would have done some things differently in these past five days if I would have known. I think you owed it to me to tell me."

BB: Well, you know what my answer is.

NDW: No, I really don't

BB: My answer is absolutely tell her and be with her when you give the news to her and stay with her.

NDW: The reason I didn't know what your answer was frankly, Brad, is because you said there are some situations where it's okay not to tell the truth, and I thought this might be one of them.

BB: There are really only two kinds of situations I can think of in which I recommend lying or withholding. The first is when you are being approached by an institutional representative such as the Nazi trooper or an FBI agent or an officer of the court. The second is where you have an agreement of confidentiality as in, for example, the therapist/client agreement, where the therapist agrees not to tell others what you said.

Since there's not an institution involved there, it's critical to the relationship between you and your mother, and your relationship to the rest of the family, and to your clarity and contact in the last moments of her life. It's absolutely critical that you tell her the complete truth and bring the doctor in and have him repeat what he said to you, to her. That's what I recommend.

And I recommend that you stay with her through whatever feelings come up and that you create a relationship like that with her before she dies—one of love and support and willingness to be with each other in facing life and in facing death. If it were you, wouldn't you like to know? I would.

NDW: Yes, of course I would.

BB: If someone has absolutely told me, "I don't want to know and I want you to absolutely not tell me if you find out," then I might make that agreement with them, because it is their choice when they're dying. If it's an agreement that you make with someone, you can do it, but then it costs you. It costs you something in relationship to that person. I recommend that people get as complete as they possibly can get with other people all the time.

But this situation of "intimacy versus managed care" is the heart of the matter about condescension, not only in situations at the end of life, but also in ongoing partnerships between couples. When people in couples merely engage in a protection racket with each other, being careful not to offend or surprise or hurt each other, it is a form of alienation that they try to pass off as intimacy. The value of the rule of thumb "tell the truth whether it hurts or offends or not" is that we grow up and grow wiser together that way. It is a union for the sake of personal growth like that one referred to so beautifully in the wedding ceremony you wrote, Neale ("The Wedding Vows from Conversations with God" by Nancy Fleming and Neale Donald Walsch, Hampton Roads 2000). For a couple to grant each other that privilege of interrupting each other's minds freely, so that they can continue to grow together, rather than be trapped in a conspiracy of minds like we were talking about a moment ago, is a wonderful thing. In other words, with regard to my intimate partner, or to my community of friends, or my whole society, am I going to contribute who I am, warts and all, and receive who they are, warts and all, so that we may learn and grow together? Or am I to remain in hiding, avoid any upset, be good and be secret and be isolated due to my carefulness not to offend? You can't ignore the warts. However, you can transform them to beauty marks in a heartbeat. The way you do that is by sharing as openly and honestly as you can.

Lying About Affairs—
Telling the Truth and Forgiveness

NDW: All right, now another one. This is the other one that often arises. It's amazing that people come up with these same kinds of problems whether I'm lecturing in Boston or San Diego.

BB: It is amazing. You know, the reason they come up with it is because they want a rationale for justifying their lying. That's what they're looking for. They've been caught.

NDW: Here's one. You find out that the husband of your best friend is having an affair, and your best friend, his wife, doesn't know it. Do you tell her?

BB: You go to him and tell him that you know and ask him if he's willing to tell her. You tell him you don't want to take away from him his right to tell her, but your knowing it now is an interruption in your relationship with your friend. Tell him that if there's anything you can do to support him in telling her the truth, you'll do it, and then, be with them while they go through the pain and the anger that it costs—be a friend to him as well as a friend to her, letting them both know that you're there to support them. Then, leave it up to him.

NDW: And if he doesn't, do you issue an ultimatum?

BB: Well, I don't know, you've got to take one situation at a time there and know more details, but you've got to keep after him. Maybe get him to read "Radical Honesty."

NDW: In my workshops I've answered the same way you just did. My answer was close to yours, and my answer goes one step further. It's a little more "radical," you might say!

You go to him once or twice. I think you give anybody three chances to do anything. After the third chance, if he doesn't do anything, you tell him: "You have thirty days to get this resolved and then I'm going to have to tell your wife, in order to maintain the integrity of who I am. I do not want your wife coming to me in five, ten or twenty years, or even five weeks, for that matter, and saying, 'How could you possibly have called yourself my friend and not let me know that you knew?' So, now, in order not to violate the integrity of who I am, I'm going to tell you that I don't really care what you do. I'm just informing you that in thirty-one days I'm going to see your wife."

BB: Good. I like that answer. Usually it works out that way in the real situations, which occur a lot. As a therapist I see a lot of these things occur and in thirty days it turns out that the truth has been told almost always anyway, without that threat. I say that there are times when you do go ahead and do it, but that you should give the person who's the primary agent in the matter as many chances as you can.

When people are in psychotherapy with me, if they're not willing to tell the truth to their spouse about an affair, I give them a little while, a couple of weeks to think about it. Then I tell them, "I'm sorry I'm not going to see you any more in psychotherapy. There's no use wasting your time and mine, because if you're not willing to tell the truth, therapy is not going to help you."

And I don't believe it does. I think a lot of psychotherapists don't know what the job is. As far as I'm concerned, the job is to help the person distinguish between what is so in the real world and their imaginings about it. If that's the job, they have to tell the truth. They have to be able to notice and report and not modify according to some bullshit idealism they learned when they grew up in whatever culture they got dumped into.

NDW: Well, you'd be a very effective therapist I would imagine, but maybe a tough one. I might feel abandoned by you and say, "Hey, don't do that to me; I need some time here. I came to you because I knew I had problems."

BB: Yes. I get that whiny response frequently—usually just before the person makes a breakthrough to honesty; then their whole life changes because they give up their victim story and their attempt to make me their victimizer.

NDW: We have a whole society though—this is what's most astonishing to me—that's built on "what you don't know won't hurt you."

BB: I know. And what you don't know hurts the hell out of you.

•••

We both agree on this. Yet here is another question we are both often asked.

"If I decide I want to start being radically honest, is it okay to say, 'From this day forward, from now on,' or do I have to look back over my shoulder? Do I have to sit down with my spouse, my brother-in law, or whoever it is, and clean it up? Do I have to tell them every thing that happened to me with regard to them in the last twenty years that I haven't told them about? Or can I just say, 'You know, Brad and Neale, I agree with you. This is a great way to live and I'm converted. I get it and I buy it and I got away with the last twenty-five years, and now I'm just going to move forward.'?"

Freud called this question an attempt not to be accountable for the past by making a new moral resolve to be good from this time forward, a "flight into health." It is a typical statement by a client acknowledging they have learned enough and are afraid to learn more. They have confessed enough, they don't want to confess more. Psychoanalysis is supposed to go on for three to five years, three times a week, and you go through this process of identifying with the therapist as your father and then as your mother and so forth. One of the things that happens is, whenever a person has a breakthrough and gets in touch with experiences, they get a little bit afraid of having too much experience and they take a flight into health. They stop coming. They suddenly say, "Thank you, Doctor, you're the greatest doctor I've ever seen. Thank you, this is a miracle cure. And now I've got to get the hell out of here!"

It's pretty similar when people get the news about radical honesty being the basis of intimacy and that without honesty there is no intimacy and without intimacy you die twenty years younger because you're not really in contact with anybody. People can suddenly have all kinds of ill-health, and all kinds of problems with their bodies and with relationships. And so they want to "get away from the original therapist." They'll find another therapist who isn't on to them yet; take up any fad or alternative they can find; keep "working on" themselves on their own; or put this book down and not come back to it for months, if ever.

Fundamentally, for your own good and the good of those around you, what you have to do is start with radical honesty. Being honest is simple. It is sometimes hard to do. But all you have to do is tell the truth about what you think, what you feel and what you have done. That's it. The whole awareness continuum can be divided into three parts: (1) what you notice outside your body right now; (2) what you notice within the confines of your skin right now; and (3) what you notice you are thinking right now. That's all. So when we speak of honesty as simple, we mean that all you have to do is report on what you notice right now. The problem that is the source of a lot of suffering is that people are constantly modifying what they report, based on thoughts about what they should or shouldn't be talking about. If they merely reported the thought "I'm worrying about _____ right now" and just continued to describe their noticing, their lives and the whole world would change. Brad and Neale both agree on that, but we do not agree on the issue of how far back to go.

●●●

BB: You absolutely have to go back and clean up the past. Everything. If you are hiding something from the past it's like having a dead horse in the living room. Everyone walks around it as though it weren't there. It rots and stinks worse every day, but you go on pretending nevertheless.

NDW: I favor something more along the lines of the Fifth Amendment approach that I talked of earlier.

BB: I definitely disagree with you and think that the "staying in charge" of your judge is the very source of alienation and role playing, and having your relationship be a performance rather than a sharing. The condescension in "not telling you because it doesn't seem appropriate to the circumstances" (for any reason, including not hurting the person unnecessarily because "after all, it is in the past and you can't do anything about it anymore anyway") is merely a rationalization for lying and preserving an illusion of being in charge. The dead horse rots. The house smells worse and worse. The whole family becomes sick from breathing the fumes.

NDW: Brad, what good does it do to go to a woman with whom you've been married for forty-seven years and tell her that in the second year of your marriage you had a weekend dalliance on that trip to Minneapolis. I mean, what else is there to do in Minneapolis? (Laughter)

What good would that do, when you know that she's going to be so deeply hurt by this? Worst-case scenario: forty-seven years of marriage, great relationship. There's been one misstep, one out-of-integrity in the forty-seven years. It was that Sunday afternoon in Minneapolis. Never happened before, never happened again.

Now you've built up this terrific relationship that is based on the level of trust she has in you, and except for this one dalliance, it wasn't altogether misplaced trust. I mean, forty-seven years, one mistake, come on. So, you feel pretty good about yourself. You've got a wonderful relationship and you realize that this lady is a very sensitive person, and she has this whole idea built up about you. She tells everyone, "In forty-seven years Bill and I have always been straight with each other." Now you've got to come forward for no reason other than that you took a Radical Honesty workshop, for God's sake. Or for no reason other than that my therapist is refusing to see me any more. He's throwing me out of his office unless I go home and say, "Esther, I've got to tell you something. Back there in '56 . . ." and she's devastated, and you know she's going to be devastated and she's not going to recover from this because her whole construction of you is based on this idea she has of who you are. And—with the exception of that one Sunday afternoon—that IS who you are. So, come on, what good does it do? What's the point? (Laughter)

BB: The problem with your story is that it has never occurred. If the person was hiding guiltily behind that withhold, then they didn't have the wonderful intimate relationship you describe and didn't tell you everything. If a person had the dalliance and lied about it in 1957, I can guarantee you that through withholding the information he or she would either feel compelled to do it again, or forever inhibited in their relationship to their spouse. There isn't any story where somebody did it once and then for forty-seven years didn't do it. Well, there may be one or two out there among the millions and millions and millions of people, but in my experience it just doesn't happen that way.

I would say yes, tell, even if it did happen that way, because right now, what makes your relationship phony is that, in your mind, *the quality of your relationship is based on you maintaining your image in your wife's mind.* You have an image about her image. Her trust is based on what you imagine she believes about you. You have to manipulate and control your image in her eyes in order to manage the relationship. And none of it's true, because something is withheld.

NDW: Can I argue with you a bit here?

BB: Sure. Go ahead.

NDW: What if your truthful reason for not telling—I mean, you go to the therapist and he hooks you up to a lie detector and he finds you're telling the truth here—is that you really are concerned with this eighty-six-year-old woman's feelings. You've gotten past worrying about what she thinks about you. I mean, my God, you're eighty-seven yourself. The truth of it is that you're saying, "Look, I just don't want to hurt her." What's the point? She's eighty-six and it happened forty-six years ago! You said yourself, Brad . . . "Use common sense."

BB: But in this case that "common sense" is a problem! It might be called common delusion instead. You've been taught that with hurt there's such a thing as irreparable damage, and there isn't. You've been taught that hurt, psychological hurt, is the same thing as physical pain and it's not. You've been taught that you're supposed to spend your whole life dancing on eggshells to make sure you don't hurt anyone's feelings. For that reason, a lot of people don't have authentic contact with other human beings. It's a big important question.

I say, *hurt people's feelings and stay with them until they get over being hurt, because you can get over being hurt in a relatively short period of time.* If it's an affair that someone you love has had with somebody, it may take you a couple of months. Most of the time you get your feelings hurt and get over it in an hour or less. Most of the time you can get really mad, really offended, and get over it within an hour or so.

If you and I were to get in a big argument, if I show up an hour late and you're mad at me, you resent me, you say, "I resent you for showing up late!" Then I say, "I resent you for resenting me!" and we holler at each other a little bit. Then, ten minutes later we go out and have a beer!

Now we're closer friends than we were before we did that. Why? Because I know that you'll tell me the truth about what you feel and you know that I'll tell you the truth about what I feel. I know I can depend on you to tell me the truth and not to condescend to me and protect my feelings as though you're the teacher and I'm the student, as though you're better and I'm worse.

Every time you condescend to someone and don't tell the truth because you think they can't take it, you're creating that world we were talking about a while ago in which you're *better* and they're *worse*. That's what causes further anger and resentment.

If I trust you to be able to handle your hurt the same way I trust me to handle my own hurt; if I authentically relate to you, I give you an opportunity to get hurt and get over it, to get mad again and get over it, and if I stay with you while you do, then I'm honoring the Being that you are much more than if I'm honoring your mind's interpretation of what has to be avoided.

NDW: I hear you and you've got to know that I agree with 99.9% of what you've said. Still, there is one tenth of one percent where I might diverge from you. There was an older woman who was in her early eighties and her husband was a little older than she was; he was eighty-six or eighty-seven. She came to a retreat because she loved the books and she brought this up. She asked, should she go home and tell Bill?

BB: Well, she'd felt guilty for forty-seven years.

NDW: I got it. I understand that. Well, even with regard to her own guilt, time heals all wounds. She's eighty-two now and she says, "Well, that happened when I was thirty-two, for heaven's sake." She's let it go.

She's let go of her guilt because she's given the guy the next forty-five years of her life in total integrity.

BB: If she really let it go she can talk to him about it. By the way, I don't agree that with regard to her guilt, "time heals all wounds." I like to say instead, "time wounds all heels." The horse continues to rot and dry up in the living room, maybe doesn't stink as bad, once mummified. But it is still blocking the way in the living room.

NDW: But her real question wasn't whether she should talk to him about it. The real question was, "How would Bill, at eighty-seven, handle that?" To make matters worse, the guy was on his deathbed and that's why he wasn't there with her at the retreat. He only had a couple of months left. She looked at me with tears in her eyes and said; "Should I tell Bill?"

Well, I've got to tell you, Brad, I said, "I don't think I would do that. I don't think I'd send him out on that note. Bill has had this fifty-two-year marriage with you and you had this dalliance when you were thirty-two. So what?"

I did say to her, "Do you need to tell him so that you can work this through for yourself? So he doesn't go and leave you feeling that you needed to tell him?" She said that she felt that she had dealt with it, resolved it, and that she had regrets but not guilt. So I asked her why she would want to tell him. She said, "That's what I'm asking you."

BB: Plus, she has wanted to tell him for all those years.

NDW: I got it. The question was should she tell him with him lying there hooked up to the oxygen waiting to die. I said, "If it were me, I wouldn't do it." What's the point? Would it be for the principle of the thing?

BB: No. No, no, no, not at all for the principle of the thing. I don't do things for principles!

NDW: (Laughter) I know that! Couldn't it be argued that the "not telling" is a greater act of love? It leaves you with the unresolved issues, after all, but you'll deal with those out of love. You'll put yourself through that rather than put the other through that.

BB: It's for the practical completion of their love of each other before he dies. He needs the opportunity to tell her about HIS two dalliances when he was thirty-seven and thirty-nine!

NDW: That assumes too much. People do sometimes have marriages where there aren't any dalliances.

BB: Yes. Sometimes they do. But, that he may have secrets he hasn't shared with her, doesn't assume too much. At least one of those two people has been holding on to a major secret all of her life. She wouldn't know if he was lying to her or not, simply because her guilt makes her listening very selective. Statistically, the odds are about 35% that he probably screwed around and lied about it too. If you interview all the married people in the United States right now, if you guarantee anonymity when you say, "Your name will not be on this form or ever associated with your answers in any way," 35% of them will tell you that they either have had, or are currently having an extramarital affair. (This is from a survey reported in the book, "The Day America Told the Truth.") Jared Diamond, the sociobiologist we mentioned earlier, who categorizes species with regard to sexual behavior, says human beings are 70% monogamous. What we know about human beings is that they have a lot of sex with each other outside of monogamy. We've known this since we've been able to do DNA testing.

As it turns out, you can go into any hospital in the world and regardless of culture, regardless of religion, regardless of where they are located on the globe, the stats tell us about 20–30% of children born were not sired by the primary male of the pair. Now, that's just the people that get pregnant when they have sex. The odds are that at least a few more have sex with protection more frequently than that, and don't get pregnant.

Genetically, just look at us for the animal that we are and don't worry about the imposition of any values whatsoever, just look at how we behave compared to how chimps behave compared to how horses behave, and you'll see that we screw around a lot.

One of the values of telling the truth is that we can start having behavior based on what is so, rather than based on some kind of thought-out hysterical projection of what ought to be so in order for us to "be good."

NDW: Well, I don't disagree with that last sentence at all.

BB: That projection of what ought to be so in order for us to "be good" is the source of our combined fury. It's the source of us having the ability to destroy the world twelve times over. Like you say, trying to be "better" than other people is the source of a lot of trouble with human beings.

NDW: I completely agree with you. I do think that there are some situations where you just say, as an act of love, that you'll carry the burden after he dies rather than have him go out on that sour note. I mean, why tell the guy on his last breath. I don't know if . . .

BB: *That's the kind of a soap opera that we all believe because we all grew up in this culture, which says that it's an act of love and sacrifice to lie to someone.* We think that if you do it for the sake of protecting their feelings that you're doing something kind and wonderful. I say you're being an idiot. You're being trapped in the jail of your own mind when you do that. I say that when you do that you're costing that person an authentic relationship with you and you're making them pay by living in an illusion. You bring them into a fantasy out of reality and you go into a fantasy and you have a fantasy relationship. So what do you want with your mate, an arrangement to avoid trouble, or intimacy? Choose.

NDW: So let's get this clear. Am I correct in saying that you think that there is really only one major exception to telling the truth, other than a confidentiality agreement that is explicit between people? That exception is where institutions are involved and the person wanting to know represents or serves as a functionary for the institution? In that case you think that not telling the truth under those conditions can be okay?

BB: Yes. Not only is it okay, but I advocate lying with great enthusiasm! Lying to Nazis can be great fun. Tell the biggest whopper you think you can get away with!

NDW: I can think of situations in which I would not offer a truth, or where I might offer a second truth over a first, such as, "I'm not wanting to discuss that right now. I don't think it makes sense to talk about that under these circumstances. And that's my truth."

BB: What I mean by the truth is the truth of experience. Not the "truth" of interpretation . . . "My truth," the way you've used it here, is the usual rationale for avoiding responsibility for saying what your interpretation is, out loud, and owning it. When you say "a truth" or "a second truth over a first" you are not referring to the truth of experience, you are referring to your interpretive mind. This is no different than the usual bullshit rationale of the habitual liar.

I disagree with this completely. I think that is pure avoidance. It is okay to delay a conversation by agreement, say in circumstances where you have to take care of work, or children, or something else first, and then talk. But to make an interpretation that "I don't think it makes sense to talk about that under these circumstances and unless the circumstances change I won't talk about it" without setting a time to talk about it as soon as possible is probably pure avoidance.

The whole heart of the matter is lying in relationship to individuals, regardless of whatever reason you might have for avoiding the truth. This is a critical disagreement. I think saying "that's my truth" or "that's your truth" is a way of simply not making the distinction between experiential truth and the interpretations of the mind. This way you avoid responsibility for reporting the truth of experience, honestly reporting what you notice is your interpretation.

NDW: We do agree on this: radical honesty does mean being willing to tell the truth to everyone about everything.

BB: Yes.

NDW: It does not mean that you must spend your time walking down the street and volunteering to the lady at the bus stop that her dress is garish, or to the guy that his aftershave is horrible.

BB: It doesn't mean that you must. But it also does not mean that you must not. You can if you want to.

NDW: It does not mean blurting out what is your own singularly experienced reality anyway (someone else might love the aftershave).

BB: Yes it does! You do report your judgments and interpretations! Otherwise you never get over them. You tell the truth about them to get over your attachment to being right, which you can't *ever* do if you're being careful not to stick out all the time or be inappropriate as you recommend.

NDW: I say it does mean living life authentically, sharing your authentic truth when and if you are asked and telling another that you would like to share your truth and will do so if they feel it might be of benefit to them.

BB: I disagree with this. It doesn't make any difference to me if it is of benefit to them in their opinion or not! It doesn't matter if they ask or not! It certainly doesn't matter whether *they think* it might benefit them or not! You are trusting your mind here, in my judgment, out of fear of trusting that telling the truth about what you feel and think may not work out, so you better manage things a little more.

NDW: It means not necessarily talking, but being *willing* to talk.

BB: No, for Christ's sake! It means talking. I think you are afraid of anger. You are, like Bill Clinton and other politicians, afraid of disapproval. In "Radical Honesty" the longest chapter in the book (53 pages)

75

is about Anger. The chapter on Anger in "Practicing Radical Honesty" is almost as long. I have lots and lots of testimonials from people who have learned how to forgive by being honest about anger because I taught them to avoid this coward's way out.

●●●

What we notice here is that Brad feels strongly about this and that Neale feels nearly as strongly. Neale does believe that there can be times when it makes sense to "take the Fifth." Brad believes that it only makes sense to Neale because he is culturally brainwashed to be a good Catholic boy and hasn't got over it yet. Neale thinks Brad is a little screwed up in the head about anger so he has to always be an extremist. Brad thinks Neale is careful out of fear. Neale thinks Brad has a nasty attitude based on unfinished business from having been lied to. They are both probably right about each other.

So it is hard to tell what you, as a reader, should do, isn't it? They are both diamonds in the rough. But it turns out that if you cut and polish them a little bit they turn out flawed anyway. Damn!

PART II

How the Truth

Sets You Free

8

Launching Honesty

In Relationships

We have both done a lot of work with couples, Brad as a licensed therapist, Neale as a spiritual counselor. Neale has been married five times. Brad has been married four times. So we might say we have seen and experienced some things over and over. One of the things we have noticed is that couples get mad at each other at times. For example, we've seen this a lot: Couples that have been married twelve or fifteen or seventeen or twenty years that are having the fourteen-year itch, or that are "getting" that their illusions about what everything was going to be like are not exactly turning out the way they expected. One of the things we notice about them is that when these couples are mad at each other, they hardly ever look at each other. They'll come in and we'll put them across from each other in the chairs. They'll speak to each other but they'll look at the floor, they'll look at the ceiling, they'll look past each other, they'll look at each other's forehead or hair or bodies, but they won't look into each other's eyes.

They haven't looked at each other, sometimes, for years. It's a successful session if, as a result of anything we do other than directly saying "look at him," or "look at her," they actually look at each other.

What Brad often suggests is that people go on a "word fast," that they spend the weekend together and don't talk. That's powerful. What happens is that they start having to pay attention to each other to tell what's going on. They report back that out of this little exercise their whole relationship has been renewed. They stopped relating to their images of each other and started actually noticing each other. Now they are ready for radical honesty.

There are other ways to launch a life of Radical Honesty right here, right now. One thing that Brad recommends is that people get a friend or a partner or a mate and say to them, "Let's make an agreement that for three weeks we'll tell each other the truth about everything. What goes on in our minds, what we feel in our bodies and what's going on with us. We'll do it as an experiment. We'll start by me telling you the truth about my past and you telling me the truth about your past." Brad invites people to tell their life stories to each other. Most folks can tell their life story in about an hour and get most of it in.

When people do tell their life stories to each other, they feel as though they've been included, brought in on something that they can't get by sharing many other things. If I'm willing to tell you what I did in my life, (including all my mistakes and all my foibles as well as all my accomplishments) and tell you what it felt like and where I screwed up (the way they tell you to in AA and other recovery programs) then I get the relief and the power to have some determination over my future. You don't have that until you go back and clean up the past. Then you have it.

You have the ability to stay off what you're addicted to because you build up your strength by telling the truth. In group work that Brad does people tell their life story to everybody in the room. They are videotaped telling the story of their life. Then they get to take those videotapes home and show them to people they're with.

Sometimes the people at home think, "I don't even know who I'm living with here," and are surprised as hell.

If you are willing to talk, you are on your way to a life of radical honesty. You don't have to take a workshop or a special program, or get private counseling to get there. All you have to do is pair up with a friend and try it. Then tell the truth about what you've done, what you think and what you feel for a couple of weeks. Once you do this, you won't want to go back to the old way of living. You'll end your game of hide and seek forever.

This time we will break into dialogue because we agree so much!

•••

NDW: You can't go back.

BB: You just don't want to. You can go back, but you don't want to, because the life that you live now is more alive than the life you've lived before you told the truth. Not all the excitement is caused by people being shocked or appalled, either. It's mostly caused by love. It's mostly caused by what we're most terrified of. I think we're more terrified of love than we are of anything else in the world. I think that we're not as terrified of anger or of sexuality. We're mostly terrified of joyfulness. We're just terrified of joyfulness. We think that if we completely love with all of our heart, we'll die. One of the reasons we live in our minds is that we can't tolerate the experience of being so completely connected with another person, so we go to our imaginations to give ourselves some relief.

NDW: I wonder if the reason we are so afraid of that love is not so much that we are afraid of the experience of love, as we are that we'll lose it. What's the point of having it if we're just going to lose it? It's like window-shopping. I can't go window-shopping.

Some people say, "One day I may want to get one of these things and I'll know exactly where it is." I know that if I'm not going to put the dollar bills on the table right then and there, I'm not going to shop. It's pointless. If I want to go buy a pair of shoes, I go buy a pair of shoes. I don't look at shoes casually for five weeks on the off-chance that some-day in the sixth week I'll want to buy a pair. To me, window-shopping is pointless.

Some people think that love, the level of love that you're talking about, that intense level of intimacy, is window-shopping. They feel that they'll never be able to have that. I know a person who just said that to my wife. They are friends, and this friend said to Nancy, "I'll never have a really intimate, long-term relationship. I'm not built for it. I just have to accept that."

There are people who actually feel that way. They believe that their past is their present. They are doomed. They are, they claim, not able to recreate themselves anew in the next grandest version of the greatest vision they ever held about Who They Are.

Others feel that even if they are able, there's no use, it will all fall apart anyway. Even if they do get it in their hands someone's going to come and snatch it away. They've been hurt so many times; they say, "Well, what's the point? I just don't want to play."

BB: You're right. Ain't it the truth! Many people feel that way. I think it comes from being little for as long as we are. We're helpless longer than any other animal. Until about three hundred years ago we had to have at least two parents in order to survive and we had to have someone take care of us for a long, long time. So we're very little and dependent and we don't have our own power and authority for a long, long time.

In the course of that time, you can't grow up without having abandonments. Growing up itself is an abandonment. I've got a seven-year-old now and I'm just resisting him getting any older. He's so sweet and he's so wonderful and we have a family bed and we sleep together and we cuddle and we snuggle and he's just wonderful. I've loved him with all my heart since he was born.

I know that as he gets to ten and eleven he's going to be a little bit more distant and a little more peer affiliated, and when he gets to be a teenager I'll just want to slap him. (Laughter)

I can feel that "going away," I'm losing him, because he's growing up, and he's losing me by growing up. I'm not going to hold him on my lap and hug him when he's nineteen years old the same way I did when he was seven. I've got a son who is twenty-four who says, "I wish you'd treat me like you do Elijah." I said, "Okay." but when he sat on my lap it wasn't the same.

So what we're afraid of is that we're going to get more of those experiences of abandonment. There's not a human being grown to adult age that hasn't had a lot of losses, that hasn't been abandoned by just growing up.

•••

In conclusion I think we can say that people get what they want. Many people *like* to complain about their partners or about the difficulties in their lives caused by other people. That means only that having a life worth complaining about is what they actually want. Werner Erhard used to say, "If you want to know what a person wants, look at what they have." We are afraid of love for all the reasons we talked about here. We are afraid of the intensity of the experience. We are afraid of losing love like we've lost it before. We are afraid of it not being returned. We are afraid of the past repeating itself and don't think we are capable of love. All these fears are obeyed because it is easier than having the courage to be. Loving is based on living out loud, and living out loud is a risk. The over-examined life is not worth living. It's better to have flunked your Wasserman test* than never to have loved at all.

---

*The blood test they give you when you get your marriage license to see if you have syphilis.

9

Noticing More

Most of us can tell when people are lying to us. And the better you are at telling the truth, the better you are at telling when someone else is lying. When you're an open book you can tell pretty easily when other people are lying.

If you've got some lies that you're propagating yourself and you're spending a lot of your energy guarding the gates, then you can't tell much about whether other people are lying or not. You just notice less. Part of the value of telling the truth is that you can notice more, and the value of noticing more is that you're here more in the world of real experience. You're alive, and when you live, you actually live the moment that you *experience,* rather than the moment that you thought that you would experience, or that you were afraid you were going to experience. You stay out of yesterday and out of tomorrow and you stay Right Here, Right Now. You stay out of Thinking and remain in Noticing.

Brad has had number of people in therapy with him who have gotten the news that they are going to die, or who came to see him when they got that news. He's carefully questioned them over the years, asking, "What was your first reaction?" Three-fourths of the people say that what they experience first is *relief.* They say, "Phew! Okay, now I can relax. Now it's over; now I know. The unanswerable question has been answered. Now I don't have to worry. I'm in charge. I'm in charge for the first time in my life. I don't have to maintain a pretense. I'm going to be dying, and it's a relief."

When people feel in charge for the first time in their lives, then they can go out and tell the truth. Someone once said that all fear is ultimately a fear of death, and that when you don't fear death any more— or at least when you're no longer afraid of when it's going to happen— then you suddenly become fearless. There's nothing left to fear.

Dr. Elisabeth Kübler-Ross once said, "There's no one more courageous than a dying man." That is true, because what have you got to lose? If you think you have nothing to lose you live each day as though it were your last. There are two ancient statements that we've all heard all our lives. They're so ancient that they're even beyond being trite. One is, "Live each day as if it were your last," and the other is, "Know the truth and the truth shall set you free." The reason those statements have been repeated over and over again is that they contain great wisdom.

Every new generation has to say those things in the colloquial language of the day, in a way that gets understood anew by the new generation. It's up to all of us to make that happen. The fact that you are reading this book right now says that you are willing to come to the edge, that you are among the leaders right now of a kind of spiritual movement that's more interested in the truth than it is in pretense.

•••

BB: I think one of the things that we want to focus on is something that I want to ask you about. How do we go about rewarding the truth and giving permission to tell the truth on a larger scale?

NDW: Oh, by getting out of "right" and "wrong." By giving up our idea of right and wrong, and, in my view, abandoning that whole system. We're making it up anyway. We should make it up a new way. I gave a talk recently and I said something the audience thought was very daring. I said, "You know, there's no such thing as right and wrong. You're making it all up generation to generation, place to place, city to city."

I had some argument from the audience about that. They said that there's got to be some absolute right and wrong. So I suggested that we pick some examples.

If a woman walks the street, in most cities on this planet, and offers certain delicious experiences to members of the opposite sex in exchange for cash, she probably will be arrested, unless the cop knows her very well, in which case he'll just get paid off—or serviced.

If he doesn't know her very well he'll take her in, because he wants the collar. She'll be arrested. On the other hand, if the same woman does the exact same thing in Amsterdam, in the Netherlands, she'll not only *not* be arrested, she'll be praised for adding to the city's tax base. In Amsterdam prostitutes are actually licensed by the government, which also grants them small business loans. That's the truth.

So, I said to the audience, "What is it, in fact, that's right or wrong, prostitution or geography? Which is it?" So we had a far-ranging discussion.

I talked about how right here in this country, in Salem, MA, not all that many generations ago we were hanging women because they were witches. We were holding up a particular book as our justification for doing that, holding up the so-called book of God, the Bible, and saying, "We hang you in the name of God because you're a witch."

I then said to the audience, "Now, if we did the same thing today, we would call the hangers, not the hangees, 'wrong'—and *we would hold up the same book in order to justify that judgment.*"

Now we're not talking about thousands of years ago, nor are we talking about Aboriginal cultures or some kind of primitive society (or what, in our judgments, we call a primitive society). We're talking about Salem, MA. Just an arm's length back across our shoulder in the past. So I said to the audience, "What's changed? It's not the stuff in the good book. We used this book to hang the women and now, a couple of hundred years later, we use this book to tell the people to stop hanging the women, and *it's the same book.*" So what's the difference?

Our point of view has changed.

We get to notice that Hemingway was right. "Life is a moveable feast."

As we evolve and have a greater sense of who we are and who we choose to be, we redefine what right and wrong is. Right and wrong is just a moving definition based on a concept of ourselves, and we're making it up as we go along.

The answer to your question, from my point of view and in my experience, is that we have to toss out even the very terms "right" and "wrong." That's what the "With God" books say. There's a whole new paradigm for living laid out in those books. Whether or not you think I talked to God is irrelevant. I experienced an interesting dialogue.

I asked God, I asked a higher consciousness in this book, "Are there highly evolved beings in the universe, and highly evolved societies?" The answer that came back was "absolutely" and that they are all over the place. I asked how they solved the problem of this floating definition of what's right and what's wrong, and back came the answer: "They don't have rights and wrongs. In fact, if you tried to use the words 'right' and 'wrong' they would look at you as if you were from some other planet (which you are), because there are no words for 'right' and 'wrong' in their vocabulary. They would wonder where you came up with this concept of right and wrong."

Well, then I asked what they use as a value system. What do they overlay upon their actions to determine what they choose to do and what they don't choose to do. I asked if they even *had* a "value system." I was told, "Oh, they absolutely do. It's what works, and what doesn't work."

And so, it's as simple and as elegant as this. Either a thing is beneficial or it's not. If you want to go to Seattle and you're driving towards San Jose, it doesn't work to head that way. That doesn't make going to San Jose "wrong," it just makes it non-beneficial. So we stop traveling in that direction.

The first step for us as a society as we evolve is to abandon our values. The people who have their feet in the mud, who are "stuck," are railing against this. They say that we are building a society without values, we are abandoning our values. Well, we are abandoning our values. We ought to abandon our values. We ought to have only one value. What is it that's working? What works? And that assessment is dependent on what it is you're trying to do.

So, when somebody says, "Well, you just have floating values," I say, "You're darn right, my values float from day to day, hour to hour and minute to minute, depending on what I'm trying to do." If I keep constant and stay clear about what I'm trying to do (for example, if I were trying to be the best possible person I can be—by my own measurement of what "best" is), and that's the beacon towards which I'm sailing, you'll see consistency in what I am calling "right" and "wrong," or "what works" and "what doesn't work."

BB: Very well said. I really love that whole last statement. That must be why so many people buy your books! Yes. That's right. That is the crux of the matter. What the mind does is convert an experience into an ideal, and once it becomes an ideal it's all mind stuff. It's a very tricky place there because you eventually convert "what works" into what's "right" and "what doesn't work" into what's "wrong." Once the word "better" enters in, you've gone into your mind, made yourself superior and someone else inferior.

With little kids, when you're open to them, you're amazed at the solutions they come up with. My little boy plays with those little plastic blocks and he builds things. He comes up with ideas about what to do with those things that would never occur to me, and they work. You watch him and say, "I wonder what he's going to do next. I wonder what the solution to this will be." If it doesn't work you might make a suggestion or he might make a suggestion, but you're not doing "right" or "wrong" there, you're doing "what works."

You're not over-valuing "what works" either. It's okay to do what doesn't work to find out that it doesn't. You can hold the value of doing what works and one of the things you're going to find out is that the way you learn to do what works is by making a lot of mistakes and doing a lot of what doesn't work. It's not wrong to make mistakes, nor is it particularly right. It's just what you do in order to be functional.

The mind loves a kind of super consistency that makes everything always be "true" all the time, in every circumstance, no matter what. It converts "what works" into "there's only one thing that works," and then you're lost. The mind can't stand the inconsistency when something works one time and not another, or just most of the time. The mind also doesn't like the messiness of mistakes and tries to avoid them—at least among people who were schooled the way we were, to count mistakes as a bad grade.

NDW: I think that as a society we're getting closer to freeing ourselves from some of those constructions.

BB: I think so, too.

PART III

Social Transformation

Through Honesty

10

Conscious Evolution

We mentioned earlier that Barbara Marx Hubbard has written a wonderful book in which she argues that throughout most of human history we've been evolving, but haven't noticed that we are involved in this process. Nor have we known for the largest portion of that time that we are, in fact, not just participating, but creating the process itself.

We touched on this before, but it bears reiterating. We are the evolved and the "evolvers." Recently many in our species have come to the conclusion that we are evolving exactly the way we are choosing to evolve. We also recognize that the process of evolution is a process of in-the-moment, here-and-now creation, not a distant participation.

One of the most exciting things about this is that the primary next step in communication to the societies of the world is that we can do this consciously. That's the communication. Now we must ask ourselves, what would happen if all of us created life, and our collective experience, deliberately rather than by chance? What would happen if we reached critical mass? That's the question. What would happen if we reached critical mass in the number of people who have committed to be conscious co-creators of our tomorrows?

The answer is that then we would truly have the world of our dreams.

There is a very distinct process now going on this planet. Anyone who looks around can see it. It is a process of the energy of conscious creation bubbling up and then spreading out, so we can reach critical mass, where more people than not are clear about what's happening and are willing to participate in the process.

We're doing this in little ways at first, taking tentative steps. Still, they are steps that can be seen by everyone, and, hence, they help all of us to believe that we can reach critical mass for longer periods, on larger issues.

There is one tiny example that took place on one evening of our collective lives, but we think that it happened consciously. We believe that the human race consciously decided how we wanted to co-create what it was going to be like on New Year's Eve of the Millennium New Year.

There was a thought in the air that this day might not go well, that there could be rebel actions or terrorist actions. And it was later revealed that there were some attempts made by terrorists to disrupt our celebration with acts of horror, but they did not succeed. The night went perfectly.

A lot of us watched the whole day, the whole twelve hours as midnight came to each part of the Earth, and we saw that unified celebration. It seems to me that there was some kind of a conscious decision, "Hey, let's not spoil this. Could we just have this one day?" It seems clear that we made that collective choice. Terrorism was prevented by our vigilance, and nothing happened.

It was a fabulous night. The Millennium New Year's Eve was our first chance as a human race to observe ourselves being ourselves at that level. There is no other time in the history of our species that we could have watched ourselves do that. It is only our advanced technologies that allowed us to observe ourselves. There never was another time before that night when everyone around the world had a chance to watch everyone else around the world. It was like the movie "Independence Day," only in reverse. It was the "un-happening" of a planetary calamity.

BB: It was like man landing on the Earth.

NDW: Exactly, exactly! We watched ourselves being ourselves and I think we all said, "Yes! Hurray!" and that's why I said earlier that I have a lot of hope that we are now ready for this process that Barbara calls "conscious evolution."

I think that something happened there. I think that the human race on that New Year's Eve *was inspired by itself.* It was inspired by its ability to conduct itself admirably: to have a good time, not to ruin it for itself, and to be, at least for one night, in a place of oneness. We watched out for ourselves, and we shared a commonality of experience.

Now we have to do the same thing again. We have to be vigilant. We have to watch out for ourselves. We made it into the 21st century, but how much farther can we go with our present mindset? That is the question before us all right now. If we are to have a chance as a species we are going to have to make some collective, species-wide decisions that can allow us to experience our oneness in many new ways. Not just in celebrating the new Millennium, but celebrating other aspects of our common experience as well.

BB: I would like to see the politicians informed of this. I'd like to see the support of public demand. I'd like for us to be making species-advantageous decisions from this consciousness. We need to be looking at other things, not just whether or not we can blow up the world twelve times before someone else blows it up four times. There's some way in which this eventually has to enter into our political experience.

NDW: A lot of people talk about the ecosystem. In "Conversations with God—Book 3" a new term was brought up: the "speciesystem." It said that what we need now is not just a healthy ecosystem, but a speciesystem that includes not just the ecology and the economy, but the political environment, the spiritual environment, the social environment, and the educational environment as well. This is the whole speciesystem, and it would get us back to what works, to what's functional, given where the species says it now wants to go and what it declares itself now to be. It's about what works and what's functional within that context. I agree with you, Brad, that we need to make those kinds of species-wide decisions and choices.

BB: I like that idea a lot. It seems to me that the health of the ecosystem, planet earth, now depends on the health of the speciesystem. Not just because there are so many of us, or because we have done, unawares, so many damaging things, but because our consciousness of what is happening and our ability to act on that consciousness is now clearly a indicating stewardship of the ecosystem of the planet. The planet will go on, of course, without us if we fail. It's just that most species as we know them today, including us, won't. *It's a kind of a race now, between the conscious and the unconscious among us.*

One of the places where consciousness is entering in right now is with regard to people and money. Businesses are becoming more sophisticated, and there are now many firms in which employees have become more conscious that their job is not just about making a buck, and that there are other considerations besides the bottom line. That's the way it's seeping into the culture. Raising our consciousness about our shared Beingness should be on the agenda of every business, in addition to the bottom line. There are more and more people who are talking about that. My friend, Dave Edwards, writer of "The Compassionate Revolution" (Green Books, 1998), and our friend Michael Lerner speaks and writes in his latest book, "Spirit Matters" and in "Tikkun Magazine" about what he calls "a new bottom line" where compassion is as honored as much as profit. Business people and corporate leaders have to be included in the decision-making process about the speciesystem and the ecosystem but the important decisions can't be made on the basis of money alone anymore.

• • •

There is a movement afoot in America and around the world to bring transparency and radical honesty to business. Many seminars and workshops are now being produced to illustrate and demonstrate how business and industry can create and use new criteria to define success and profit. In these seminars, leading-edge management techniques are taught, exploring models used by successful companies right now in which there is a high level of participatory decision-making on company policy, goals, budgets, salaries, hiring, product development, and other management and administrative options.

In "Conversations with God—Book 2," a whole section was devoted to the concept of transparency, as it would apply to the business community and our economic interactions with each other. The text lays out a hypothesis that says that everything would change remarkably for the better if businesses simply decided to be utterly and completely transparent in their interactions—with each other corporately, with their customers, and with their own employees.

Brad operates both a for-profit and a non-profit corporation where "All Is Known" is the motto. Nothing is secret. Everything is revealed in detail and all books are open. Brad has also founded a new nation on the Internet called "The United States of Being," the border of which is the atmosphere of the earth. (The tee-shirt says, "U.S.O.B!") Also, his non-profit company, The Center for Radical Honesty, sponsors a program once a year called "The Thought Leaders Course in Honesty," where sixteen business leaders, artists, writers, seminar leaders, etc. convene for eight days and take the course in honesty together. Out of this "The World Council for the Transition to Compassion" is forming, and at regular meetings of this group, twice a year, they will review and discuss how conscious participation in the speciesytem's evolution can occur.

This is all based first and foremost on people sharing honestly about everything they are about in the world. Let's look at an example of the kind of transparency we're talking about here. At this level of transparency every company and every corporation would distribute a piece of paper to every employee once a month listing the compensation package of everybody in that employee family. We're not talking about salary ranges, like, "Jim makes from $35–$46K per year," but to-the-penny salaries—what everyone makes, what their benefits package is, what their stock options are, literally everything that is true for everybody in the corporation, from the door keeper to the chairperson of the board.

Neale has been bringing this up at public lectures lately and he reports that some members of his audience—usually male—just get up and leave. Others become agitated and say, "That's just not practical. We can't do that. Besides, that's nobody's business." These are the top guys saying this, of course.

Neale does this right now at Greatest Visions, and at the ReCreation Foundation, the non-profit organization that he and his wife created. Every month at the staff meeting out comes the piece of paper and the employees get to deal with all the stuff that comes up for them around that.

Someone might say, "Oh, Janice got a raise, well." Neale has been asked very directly, "How come Janice makes $32,600 and I make $25,900 and we're both doing the same kind of job, and furthermore, I've been here four months longer than she has?"

When you operate your business in transparency you've got to explain your rationale and be up front. You've got to say to that person, "I can tell you that, if you really want to know. The answer is that she does a better job than you. She's not afraid of putting in a few hours overtime, she does what she's asked more quickly, she's more conscientious and, frankly, she's a more valued employee. That's the truth of it. It's not that you aren't valued at all. If you were not valued, you wouldn't be here. But your respective value to us is not the same. If you want to learn how to make $32,600 instead of $25,900, talk to Janice."

Neale's managers have those kinds of conversations at their staff meetings all the time, and the level of health—we're talking about mental and emotional health here, which translates into vibrancy within the staff—is remarkable as a direct result of those conversations. The main argument against transparency is that no one would put up with the truth. That's a very sad argument, and it is just not true.

Neale knows of a construction firm in San Diego that took him up on this. The owner of the firm began to release the salaries of all of his employees and he also began to tell every one of his customers how much his subcontractors and suppliers were charging him for that bucket of nails and that hour of electrical work. He passed that information right on to the customer. He told them that the guy who did the electrical work charged him $45 per hour and that he was charging them $65 per hour. It's right there. The customer would ask why would you want to charge me that $20, and he would explain it all and tell the customer what that money was used to maintain. He was so afraid to do this, yet he risked his company's profitability to try this and by doing so he tripled his company's profitability in eighteen months.

When he called to report that he said, "This is what I'm commonly hearing from people—the word on the street is that they're recommending me to everyone who wants home remodeling done. They're saying that if this guy is that honest and that open, that's the guy I want to build my house. If he's coming from that level of integrity he'll do a good job, and if he doesn't do a good job, he'll tell you 'we blew it' and do it again."

The word-of-mouth business he got was incredible. His bottom line has tripled out of his willingness to come clean and be that straight up, and to say, "Yeah, that bucket of nails cost me $12, I'm charging you $30, and that's what's true."

Brad has a number of stories of success in business in "The Truthtellers: Stories of Success by Honest People." He and his colleagues intend make "The Truthtellers" a series of books and tapes to keep telling these wonderful stories as they happen. They are intended to inspire and encourage people to try openness and transparency rather than secretiveness, and bluffing, and sales pitches, and competition through withholding. He had an interesting story of his own in response to Neale's story about how his friend's honesty in business paid off.

•••

BB: I'd much rather personally deal with someone like that, who shoots straight from the beginning. I actually had the experience of building my own house about ten years ago. I was my own general contractor and helped design the house. I had about a hundred sub-contractors over the course of six months. I was the only general contractor I knew of at the time who actually started a job and completed it in six months just as planned. I said I was moving in November 1st and I did. I did the whole project as an experiment in conscious intention.

It happened because of the quality of communication I had with every sub-contractor. I told them the truth about what I wanted and how I could support them. I said, "I've also talked to two other plumbers and every day you don't show up, you're going to be behind me on the money and I'm not going to pay you your money, I'm going to pay it to somebody else to do that job. If we're going to have an argument, we're

going to have it up front, right now. I want us to have the communication necessary that allows you to do what you want to do for a living and
me to support you, and to have you support me in building a house."

I talked about how "you're supporting me and I'm supporting you
and we're working together on this." I told them that I had been in
business for myself for a number of years and had also done some construction work and that I knew what it was like to try to run a business.
I told them I would call them a specified number of days prior to the days
I would need them, and we agreed on the number of days notice they
wanted. I said that I expected them to stay on the job once they were
started until it was completed and not move their people to other jobs
and leave me out even if they had other jobs going at the same time. I
told them that I knew they understood that my job was mostly coordi-
nating things, so that once the plumber was finished the electrician could
come in and then the insulation man and then the wallboard man, etc.
And that a delay caused by one person not doing this job when he said
he would do it, could throw the whole project off schedule.

Then, I said again to them that I would give them a small portion of
money to start their contract with me and then would stay behind them
on paying the money until their job was completed; if they fell behind I
would replace them and give the money to the other guy and not pay
them. I said that if we were going to have any conflict about that, let's
have it right now.

And then I listened to them. We got clear about our agreements
and about how life is short and we all need to have as good a time as we
can while we work and we all have to help each other, and depend on
each other and tell each other the truth about what goes on and not
bullshit each other.

Then I asked them what time they usually got up in the mornings
and they told me, and I said I would call them at that time or a little
earlier each day they were supposed to be on my job to support them in
getting there. I said I would find out if they needed me go for parts or
supplies, or if they needed anything else from me.

A lot of those folks were and still are my neighbors where I live out in
the country and some of them are still friends of mine today. They were

very kind to me and helped me beyond the call of duty and we did have a good time building that house. In some cases we did occasionally have conflict, but we settled it face-to-face in the context of our agreements. They brought their families out to see what they were working on and to meet me and to celebrate our work together. We were proud of what we had done, not just the house, but the way we made it happen.

NDW: It was more than just a job at that point.

BB: Yes, it was a lot more than just a job.

NDW: We don't see that this IS radical honesty. Not just radical honesty across the dinner table or across the bed with your loved one or your beloved. This is the possibility for high-level radical honesty in the corporate boardrooms of America.

BB: I know and you know and a lot of other people are learning that what allows people to have new, unique, creative and powerful perspectives is being clear with their attention, and with their intention, which requires that they be honest. What this ultimately comes to is that the *secret of profitability in an information age is honesty.*

NDW: You know, we're getting to the point where one day it's almost going to become impossible *not* to be honest, given the incredible traffic of information.

BB: I hope so. It would be a big relief. This adolescent game of constantly working to maintain your image, to control the way people feel about you, to hype things in the media in order to sell things in order to be profitable, is going by-the-by. It's receding. People are more interested in the way things really are than ever before. This is true in business on a personal level, and it is becoming true on a corporate level.

Every human being that I've ever met is really vitally interested in knowing what life is really like for those other people over there, and asks, "Is the way that my life is, the same way that your life is?" They really are interested in the truth.

That's the most hopeful thing for me. I know that everyone is interested in the truth and that everybody wants to make a contribution to other people. I've seen people in prisons, in mental hospital, and on the street, and I've never met a human being that didn't fundamentally want to make a contribution to other human beings. I never met a human being that wasn't fundamentally interested in the question, "What's it like over there?"

NDW: I agree with you. I never met an individual who didn't want fundamentally to be honest, if he thought he could get away with it. Yet what's true for individuals does not seem to be true for groups of individuals when they get together in a clan or a society or a corporation or some kind of special environment. For example, no individual doctor, or at least very few individual doctors, holds the same point of view as the American Medical Association.

BB: I know. In the civil rights movement they polled restaurant owners in the South during the height of all our sit-ins and theater stand-ins. They found out that 70% of restaurant owners did not believe in segregation and in fact believed in desegregation, but said they didn't think they could afford to publicly support it because they'd lose their businesses. They said this because they believed that most of the other people in the community didn't believe in desegregation. As it turns out, if you surveyed the other people, the percentage was about the same as the business owners. Segregation existed as a tradition way beyond the belief that sustained it. I think that when people establish traditions in large groups it just takes them a hell of a lot longer to get over outmoded systems than it does individuals. Of course, there is always support in such groups for individuals to retreat to when on the edge of breakthroughs in thinking, because the group wants the older traditions reinforced and maintained.

NDW: Certain behaviors have become institutionalized and so continue, even though the individuals who created and supported that institution being in place no longer hold that belief. The question is, "How do we bridge the gap so that the integrity and the wishes and desires of individuals bubble up and disintegrate institutions and recreate them?"

BB: The institutions are the parallel to the mind. The institution on the social level is the same thing as the mind on the individual level. If there is a parallel between the mind of the individual and the institution of the society, the parallel is that they want to do things the way they've been done before. The mind likes to keep consistent and an institution likes to keep things consistent, regardless of how outdated it is or how irrelevant it is to the facts and the territory.

The linguist and philosopher, whose name I can't recall right now, who said, "The map is not the territory," gave a map to a group of people at a meeting in London and he told them to enjoy themselves in town and then come back in a couple hours for further discussion. He in fact had given them a map of Moscow. (Laughter) So they actually had the experience of walking around London trying to find things with a map of Moscow. When they came back he said, "So you see, it's relatively important that the map fit the territory."

The problem with our minds and the problem with our institutions is this: the map is no longer fitting the territory. The territory changes and the map doesn't work, but we keep on using the same map.

The question is, "How do you get over belief?" And the answer is that you first have to understand that belief itself, regardless of what the belief is, or whether it's about something "good" or something "bad," once held in opposition to reality, is a kind of avoidance of reality. We like to hold on to beliefs way beyond their application to reality. Alan Watts wrote a book entitled "The Wisdom of Insecurity" in which he said that life is like a river and to actually be secure you need a boat. But people don't like boats because a boat doesn't "feel secure." He said most people try to put a post in the riverbed to hold on to, and even when floods come and the river beats the hell out of them, they hold on to their post because they want to feel safe and secure, even though they aren't. I think that the fundamental Buddhist idea that attachment to belief is the most universal cause of suffering is correct. It also explains, I think, why the largest economic enterprise on Planet Earth is illegal drugs (most of them painkillers). One of the largest legal corporate enterprises in the world is called the pharmaceutical industry, manufacturing primarily anti-depressants, painkillers and the like. The question arises, "Why do we need so many pain killers?" The simplest answer is, "Because there is a lot of pain!" I think most of the pain comes from holding onto that post in the riverbed of life, called "belief," while life beats the hell out of you for your ill-fitting models of reality.

•••

For years Neale has been saying in his lectures that what we have to do is change our belief system, our cultural story. That's really what we're talking about here. We have to change our whole cultural story. In "Communion with God" it says that the problem with the human race is that we are living our lives not according to the Ten Commandments, but according to the Ten Illusions. These ten illusions have created our cultural story. Among them are the illusion that need exists, the illusion that failure exists, the illusion that separation exists, and the illusion that insufficiency exists.

None of these illusions are real. They seem real, and they are not real. Sometimes there's a conflict between the experience of what you notice and what you think you ought to be seeing. Either one of those is resolvable by paying more attention, or by heightened awareness. These are what resolve apparent logical contradictions because awareness transcends the mind, which has to operate according to dichotomies.

Psychotherapy is a place where this shows up. Every single individual suffering is caused by someone being trapped in one dichotomy or another and therefore not being able to see what is so. They can't actually acknowledge what is so because they're trapped in their mind about what they ought to be thinking about it, "the way it ought to be."

As we deal with each other in honesty, what we do is give each other permission to not have to be right, permission to be confused and permission to not have to be happy all the time. It's such a relief. We're all in this boat together. When we know this we see that there's a kind of communication between people that just has to be honest. It's honest because once we've already revealed the thing that's most taboo, like our confusion, uncertainty, or unhappiness, etc., we are free to talk about anything whatsoever after that.

• • •

BB: At the end of my workshops we do an "ideal world statement." I use this thing from Phil Laut, who's an author who wrote a book about money. He has this exercise where people come up with the purpose of their life. First they write a list of personal characteristics, then a list of past specific behaviors that are evidence that those characteristics are accurate. The instructions are sequenced in such a way that the lists trick the participants into writing a statement of purpose for their lives. They merely answer questions and do the simple task of making lists, instead of trying to figure out what they "should" do with their lives. Then they write their vision of an ideal world. It just says, "An ideal world is one in which . . ." and they fill it in.

So there are sixteen people at the end of these workshops that all write up their vision of the way they want the world to be. What blows their minds and mine too all the time, and it happens over and over again, is that almost everyone's vision of an ideal world is the same. It's almost exactly the same. Even the wording is the same. It has to do with some sense of responsibility for the planet, establishing ecological balance, wanting people to be happy, and wanting people to have enough food to eat, and having adequate shelter.

Those kinds of things are commonly owned as ideals by every person who's come to my workshops, which is a fair cross-sectional sample of mostly middle-class America. Basically, a lot of people agree on the way they would like to see the world be and yet at the same time, as we were saying a while ago, it somehow doesn't come into being.

NDW: Well, because they can't agree on how to get from here to there.

BB: That's right, it's just a matter of how to get from here to there.

NDW: Methodology. The disagreement on methodology has created a lack of ability to reach the place where we do all share a common agreement, because we don't know how to get from where we are to where we want to be.

I think that the first step, getting back to Barbara Marx Hubbard, is realizing the fact that we are participatory players in the game. We're not on the sidelines watching ourselves get where we want to be but, in fact, it is out of our own thoughts and decisions and choices and intentions that the whole process of evolution arises.

I think there is some hope, because we're now seeing this. We're saying, "Oh, I get it. I get it. It's this way because I made it like this. *I made it like this.*"

There are now enough of us agreeing about this, and that's a new place for the human race to be.

BB: It's being responsible instead of being guilty. It's noticing instead of thinking. It's being present to experience rather than in your mind about what ought to be. When we focus on creating with our minds instead of shaming ourselves with our minds, and we honestly share everything we come up with then a whole new life together is possible. Taking responsibility is so much more fun than guilt!

NDW: Responsibility erases guilt, because responsibility at least allows us to notice that we made that choice intentionally. It's very difficult to be guilty about something you did intentionally.

BB: Right. You can say, "I'm sorry I did it" but you don't feel bad.

●●●

Having guilt, or shame or regret is mostly a waste of time and is not the same as taking responsibility for our actions.

We think that honesty allows for a clearing, where people can acknowledge what is so, including their part in making what is so be the way that it is. Then, mutually constructive rebuilding can occur.

11

Social Transformation:

The Undoing of a System

Of Secret Influence

In order to protest campaign finance corruption Brad intentionally got arrested, twice—with two small groups of people who were members of the Alliance for Democracy—in the Rotunda of the Capitol building in Washington, D.C. This is what he said about it.

•••

We called ourselves the *Freedom Brigade.* We were supported by a number of other people from The Alliance for Democracy. We were trying to keep alive the conversation about the way campaigns are financed in this country. In order to control legislation, millions of dollars in campaign contributions have come from industry groups. For instance, at that time about thirteen million dollars had come from the oil industry; about eleven million dollars from the insurance industry; and approximately thirty other industries had donated more than ten million dollars each.

We began our protest by revealing all that information with handouts and articles and personal conversations to contribute to and expand the dialogue about campaign finance reform in late 1999 and again in early 2000. We assembled in the Rotunda, forcing the police to arrest us, in order to draw attention to the issue.

The conversations in the paddy wagon and in jail and in the courtroom showed that those of us who participated in this social action did so out of our own individual transformations and out of our compassion—out of our identification with other human beings. Because we had learned some things about who we were, both good and bad things, we understood more about how people can both be wonderful and also be screwed up. We protested the screwed upness of the few who were hurting the many. We were protesting that some screwed up people have a lot more power than the rest of the screwed up people. We were for equal opportunity screwedupedness—a thing called democracy. It ain't much, but it's better than the plutocracy we currently have.

A month or so after we were arrested and released we went to trial. There we learned more about the relationship between individual and social transformation.

In April of 2001 the McCain/Feingold campaign finance reform bill passed the Senate, fifteen months after our protests to bring the subject to public attention. At this writing the bill has still not cleared the house. What is proposed in that bill is still a far cry from full public financing. If it does pass, it will make it a little harder for multi-national corporations to keep their bribes secret, and will somewhat limit how much they can pay. Even that modest attempt at reform may never pass because of the degree of obligation of those in Congress to people who have paid for their election campaigns.

In this chapter, Neale and I decided to include an article I wrote describing the testimony at the trial of participants in this particular social reform because we think that one important manifestation of spiritual growth is compassion in action. It is clear from people's testimony that their willingness to act to change the laws about campaign financing is based on their own spiritual growth, and that compassion for others and love of their families is a central consideration.

I got arrested because I believe that there is a relationship between personal freedom from the mind and social freedom from domination by institutions. The protest my friends and I made was against secret alliances of institutions of influence to elect candidates. I wrote the article that follows because I thought that the testimony of all of us eloquently expressed a vital point of view. It also shows how individuals committed to having the truth be known can begin to hold the government accountable for being open and honest and telling the truth.

Criminal Justice:
Hey! That's a Good Name for It!

The first arrests happened in October of 1999 when Ronnie Dugger, founder of the Alliance for Democracy and seven others held up signs and spoke in loud voices in the Rotunda of the Capitol building in Washington about democracy being for sale. Then, six more of us got arrested in January, a part of the Democracy Brigade started by the Alliance for Democracy. We got ourselves arrested to protest the way campaigns are financed by multi-national corporations, giving them undue influence. That is called a plutocracy. We wanted that issue talked about and revealed to everyone in the country in hopes that democracy; another faulty, though more honest, form of government might prevail.

We were arrested the first time in 2000, in the last week in January. Then, a third Democracy Brigade made up of sixteen of us got arrested in the Rotunda again on February 29, leap year. In March most of the last arrest group went to trial—fourteen friends, all guilty of the same offence. (Two of our number couldn't make it to the first trial date set and had to get postponements to a later date.)

I was guilty. I pled guilty. But I didn't feel guilty. I had a hell of a good time being guilty and I fell in love with a bunch of people and felt really good about myself and I think most of us did, and I want to tell you about it. It feels good to take a stand for the truth.

We all got to enter a plea of guilty and testify briefly about why we broke the law. What follows are excerpts from the transcript of the court record of our testimony and the judge's response and a bit of the story of what occurred.

Superior Court of the District of Columbia

March 23, 2000

"Mr. Blanton?"

THE WITNESS: I'm Dr. Brad Blanton. I'm the author of a book called "Radical Honesty." I have been a clinical psychologist in Washington, D.C. for the last twenty-five years. I was demonstrating in the Capitol against campaign finance corruption in protest of the way the world economic order works.

If we were to take the whole population of the world and reduce it to a group of one hundred people in a room, with all ratios remaining the same, of the hundred people in the room, eighty of them would be ill-housed, fifty of them would be suffering from malnutrition and ill-nesses related to malnutrition, seventy of them would be unable to read, one would have a college degree, one would own a computer, and six of them would control enough of the resources to essentially control the rest of the people in the room. All six of the rich people would be citizens of the United States of America.

It seems to me that if we were, in fact, in a room with a hundred people and we got to know each other and see each other and talk to each other and smell each other, that we would probably get these problems handled—because normal human compassion would come into effect after people actually experienced each other. But with over six billion people on the planet, what maintains the conditions that keep these circumstances in place is the primary valuing of the bottom line. The people who have the money can afford to buy the legislation necessary to do just that—maintain the bottom line as a primary value. They do that through financing campaigns for people elected to public office and by constantly influencing them with paid lobbyists.

So campaign finance reform to me is *critical* to being *actually* compassionate rather than some kind of phony compassion that's part of the current political dialogue. So I'm proud to plead guilty. I am guilty as charged for demonstrating in the Capitol Rotunda against campaign finance corruption.

•••

It was late in the day and the judge had been kind enough to have us seated in the empty jury box, rather than forcing all of us to remain standing while each person testified. The judge, named Weissberg, a distinguished looking middle-aged, graying man, had just addressed each one of us personally, one at a time, asking us a series of questions. He asked each of us if we were sober, and not under the influence of drugs. He asked if we clearly understood that if we entered a plea of guilty we could get six months in prison and a $500 fine or both. We all said, one at a time, that we understood. Then we were allowed to testify. He asked us to try to keep it under two minutes. I got to speak first because my last name starts with a B.

When it came our turn to testify, each of us stood up when we spoke, and sat down again when we finished. We ranged in age from eighteen to seventy-six. Somehow in that controlled and formal setting, in that big hollow courtroom, and that great range of age, the words each of us spoke to account for why we were there, had a kind of declarative, definitive ring, and a cumulative effect, like an inscription on a tombstone.

Our attorney was polite but persistent (he wasn't in the American Civil Liberties Union for nothing). The judge, you could tell, was overloaded and a little tired, but happy to have a reprieve from much more boring work. Even the government prosecutor was actually paying attention to what we said. We "guilties" were all in love with each other for being brave enough to get there. As we listened to each other speak, some of us cried. Even the judge was moved by what we said. As we continued to speak, more and more clarity about what we were actually doing there seemed to emerge. Democracy happened.

As each person's name was called out it seemed like a roll call of nationalities. We had last names that showed that our little jury box, melting-pot family were sourced from all over Europe, and several of us had blood in our veins from native America as well. These are only brief excerpts but they give some sense of what was said and what it was like to be there:

"Mr. Conant?"

"We did not risk arrest lightly, but from the sense that to speak truth to power in the Capitol was our civic responsibility, an action not disrespectful for our country, but rather undertaken from a profound love of it—from the passionate love of the principles on which it was founded and out of the deep fear that these principles are increasingly subverted by the corrupt system which makes Congress far more responsive to the needs of corporate donors than to the people."

"Ms. Cusimano?"

"I would like to pass on a better way of voting for my daughter and children."

"Mr. Cusimano?"

"My family, my friends and neighbors, voting members of our nation have lost faith in our representation of our Government. True Statesmen are left out of the political arena, along with the people's concerns, needs and desires. We, the people, want our Government back. We, the people, want our country, our democracy back for ourselves and for our children."

"Mr. Demere?"

"Your Honor, I have ten grandchildren. I'm concerned about their future, the kind of nation they will inherit. The power of money that exerts pressure on politicians eats away at the health of our society. Behind many of our social ills lies the infamous influence of big money on the affairs of state."

When Mr. Demere the elder sat down, his son David was called upon.

"Mr. David Demere?"

"One of his ten grandchildren (nodding at his father), is my daughter who's now seventeen, Laquisha Demere, and I named her in honor of Laquisha Mott whose statue is there in the Rotunda. I brought my daughter there seven years ago to look at that sculpture. I named her Laquisha because I wanted her to have the same kind of conviction that Laquisha Mott had for justice and fairness and equality. That is why I stood in the shadow of Laquisha Mott in the Rotunda with the other sixteen activists acting out of conscience in an effort to expose and change the corporate-oriented big money campaign system we have in our beloved country."

"Mr. Hanmann?"

"That great domed space is replete with pictures and sculptures of history and heroes, it is presumed to be a museum. But when I entered the Rotunda on February 29th, I thought I was on the stage of democracy. I misbehaved in the museum of our history in order to confront our future. So the rotunda was for me a platform, a stage on which I sought redress of my grievances and where I claimed the right of free expression and free speech at the very hub of Government . . . there to protest the political commerce that displaces a Government of ordinary people with the Government of special money."

"Ms. Kenler?"

"Your Honor, I have just a bit of hope left that the state of our earth and the health of all the creatures on it can be helped by our actions. And I really do believe that full public financing of campaigns could bring about what most people want, which is a good life, and this is the best I can do to take that responsibility for myself and for my family and my community."

"Mr. McMichael?"

"We know that unless they're restrained in the political employment of their wealth, experience shows that the wealthy will come to dominate the society to the great detriment of the non-wealthy, who in all societies are the great majority."

"Ms. Parry?"

"I do not come here lightly. I do not want to be here. Nor did I want to have to demonstrate in the Capitol Rotunda. I had no wish to be arrested.

I went to the rotunda on February 29th to redress my grievances with Congress because they are not listening and the media is not reporting. I went, Your Honor, because I believe in my deepest of hearts that our democracy is at stake."

"Mr. Price?"

"Unless I openly state my grievances against the democracy-killing effects of corporate money in the legislative and electoral processes, I will have, through my silence, negated the sacrifices of democracy's heroes, including those of my father who served in Germany in World War II."

"Mr. Silver?"

"I think the folks here have summed it up. This is the reform that has to happen in order to make any other reform possible. And it's the only issue I would do this for. And I do it with great pride."

"Mr. Stanton?"

"In 1931, April Crawford and Arnold Stanton came to Washington, D.C. from North Carolina to get married. They got married at the Washington Monument. They believed in this country. They believed in democracy. They had hopes. Almost seventy years later, I come to the Rotunda, their son, because I have to speak out because I feel like my democracy has gone. A lot has happened in those seventy years. Most of what has happened has done more and more to disenfranchise us. I don't want my grandsons to come here and do the sort of things I did at this time to get attention to get the Government back to the beat."

After Mr. Stanton, the judge took his turn to speak. This is just my opinion, but I think he was aware that he was speaking into a listening created by us, and that it was a listening worth speaking into, *and that he wanted to actually thank us for being who we were.*

"I took guilty pleas yesterday or the day before from a much smaller group, I think four people who were demonstrating for a different cause under slightly different circumstances. And I used the opportunity to engage them as best I could, about what it was they were here for and who they were when they were not here. And to some extent, to debate them about some issues that I felt were relevant—although not on the merits of their cause. I would enjoy the opportunity to do that with you folks because you are all obviously very passionate about what you believe in and committed to this issue, and also very articulate in expressing your point of view.

"And if this were a different forum and if time permitted it, I think I would enjoy the intellectual stimulation of getting to know you better and maybe even playing devil's advocate on some issues. But I think that would be self-indulgent on my part at this point. And it's late and I don't think we can do that.

"It seems to me the sentence suggested by your attorney is a fair one. You've spent five hours of some indignity paying a price for doing what you did, and I don't see any need to exact a higher penalty. Although there is an addition to that. A cost of $50 which is obligatory . . . mandatory under the statute for the victims of violent crime compensation fund which every person convicted has to contribute to, so that people who are victimized by crime and cannot afford to pay the cost of their injury can have some fund to draw on to help defray those costs. So that's what I intend to do.

"The only thing I would add is something that I talked about the other day with the other four. And that is that what I'm not sure of as a judge, and I've been doing this a long time, and I've also dealt with a lot of, if I can use the term, demonstrator arrests or demonstration arrests. But what I haven't really thought through clearly in my own mind is whether there should be an escalating price if someone's conscience compels them to come back again and again and we have to drop everything and conduct court for them as we do. Whether there's a rule for deterrence and whether it's even a proper consideration for sentencing in court for a criminal act such as this.

"I don't know how I'll resolve that, but I state it only as sort of a something for you to think about. And maybe as a warning because all of you are obviously so passionate about what you believe in that there may well come a time, whether on this issue or some other issue, your conscience will bring you back to Washington in some other form of demonstration and there will be another arrest. And if there is, if the judge before whom you appear feels that the proper thing to do, having gotten essentially a—I don't mean this in a demeaning way—but having gotten essentially a free pass the first time, there should be a higher price to pay the second time, then you should prepare yourselves for that.

"Because you all know, and one of the reasons I'm required by law to tell you about it before I take your plea, is that when you do this sort of thing, the maximum price you could be asked to pay would be six months in jail or a $500 fine, or both. And that is a very steep price and one needs to know that before they decide how to conduct their affairs.

"Having said that, the sentence for all fourteen of you is what I'll call time served, which is intended to reflect the five hours that you were held before you were released and a requirement that you pay $50 to the victims of violent crime compensation fund, which is payable in the finance office in Room 4203.

"Thank you. You can all be excused. As soon as we—you will have to wait until we give you this form which you take with you to pay the $50 in the finance office and then you're free to leave."

We appreciated him for what he said. We liked him. He liked us. The truth is, even in that sterile place, in that stale and antiquated system, that completely deadened context where the dead law usually bores people to tears, for the time being, for the moment, at least, a spirit of compassion was around. Everyone in the room had been touched by each other's presence and each other's words and we were in a place of community and we were happy—and the judge just couldn't leave after we were through! And we didn't want to leave either! He stayed and talked with us for twenty minutes after the trial was over and was, I believe, actually honored to be with us.

Another Day, Another Judge

A week or so later, one of our colleagues, who couldn't make it to court with us that day, got another judge on another day, who did not allow her to testify on her own behalf whatsoever, and sentenced her to five days in jail and the maximum $500 fine. That penalty was for the same offence we had committed, right beside her, on the same day, at the same time.

There are two things you can say about the courts and the criminal justice system: (1) What happens to you still mostly depends on the judge you get and the mood they are in. (2) The Criminal Justice System is well named.

Commitment to changing the arbitrariness of that system clearly has to be part of what we, who are interested in honesty and fairness, are about.

The judge our group had was an exception, and stood out because of it. The judge our friend got was pretty much just doing her job as a hireling of the corporate *status quo* we were protesting in the first place.

In the transcript of our trial the court reporter kept substituting the word "conscious" for the word "conscience" spoken by the judge, and the mistake was more than just entertaining. I think consciousness requires that we transcend the limitations of the law and the courts by choosing how we behave independently, and separate from the system, and that we do not cooperate with it out of fear. Somehow we have to learn how to be able to love a bad judge in a bad mood, on a bad day without honoring a dishonorable system. Come to think of it, that is pretty much the same thing it takes for most of us to get along with each other and ourselves, about half the time anyway. To love the being I am, in spite of my mind, is why I meditate. That seems a direct analog to loving a variety of judges in a variety of moods but not honoring in the slightest the crap they come up with.

Compassion for ourselves and compassion for others must be achieved independent of the shoulds of our individual minds and the bad laws and systems of society. It has to be worked out in the heart and in the world through honest self-expression and a change of heart. We have to raise hell and fight and yell and write until we can work through to a place of forgiveness of others and ourselves in order to have the power to change the world. So I am going back to the Capitol Rotunda again to learn some more about that. Individual transformation and social transformation can't really be separated. You can't have one without the other.

We were lucky this time—most of us. We got a good judge on a good day this time around. We got a chance to speak up and make our point to get to know each other and publish this story. And we got off with just "time served." Maybe we'll be lucky again. Who knows?

This appears to be how social change occurs: everyone gets busted, including not just us who have the papers to show for it, but also the cops and the court system, the politicians, the businesspeople, the lobbyists and those of you who haven't shown up yet. Getting busted and acknowledgment of it is the first step toward getting over old models of the mind. Old models of the mind that don't fit reality anymore, on the *individual* human level, are called ignorance, and are the source of suffering. Old models of the mind that don't fit reality anymore on the *social* level are called tradition, heritage, necessity, or the law, and are also the source of suffering. The very tough process of getting mad and getting over it, or getting hurt and getting over it, getting busted and getting over it, being treated unfairly and getting over it, is necessary, so that antiquated systems of thought and governance can be dispensed with. It is called forgiveness. Forgiveness leads to compassion and *vice versa.* Compassion leads to freedom. Lucky for us, there is a lot to forgive out there.

The process itself may require telling a judge to go to hell somewhere along the way, or a corporation to discorporate, but that's what we created a democratic society for in the first place, wasn't it? I think we are all learning, individually and together. I think we will, someday soon, have justice prevail and compassion win out and forgiveness become possible. I can see us all marching down the corridors of justice, singing about the simultaneity of individual and social transformation . . . "You can't have one, no you can't have none, you can't have one without the o-o-other." Most people probably won't know what in the hell we are singing about, but it is a big part of our job to tell them until they get it. Individual transformation and social transformation happen at the same time.

12

Honesty in Business

And Commerce

In the businesses that actually have consultants come in to teach them how to tell the truth more, the people involved are very, very unlikely to become transparent in the way that we advocate because the whole system, they believe, depends on secrecy. They believe, that the worldwide economic order depends on secrets. It depends on the competition that comes from trying to get there first and getting there first because the other guy doesn't know what you're doing. That model is an outdated institution. It's no longer applicable but it's still being used.

• • •

NDW: There's a company now, in England, that's trying to get to the bottom of understanding the mapping of our genes. I'm sure you've read about it. They're releasing all of their research day by day as they make their new discoveries.

BB: They turn it loose to everyone.

NDW: There's another firm in Washington, D.C., an American firm, which is on the same track, trying to release and unleash the genetic code of the human being. They're doing it privately. They've been challenged by the worldwide press, which asked, "Why don't you do what the group in England is doing?" The company has come right out (and you have to give them credit for that) and said, "We're in this for profit and we have to not release this information because we want to be able to get a patent and a trademark on this."

Let's talk about the practicality of this kind of honesty and transparency in business. How would you for instance, get a patent and a trademark on something if you were releasing research data as you went along?

BB: I think you can do both/and rather than either/or.

NDW: How would you have a competitive edge? How would you? You would lose the competitive edge if you told everyone what you were doing.

BB: Maybe, maybe not. You see you could have a trademark and a patent for a limited period of time to produce it exclusively without having to keep it secret. There are ways to work this out. My first thought on it is to let people still have an exclusive temporary right, or let them have their temporary monopoly. That's what they're going to get anyway. Why not give them that and then say, "But you let it go as you find it out."

So then other people can go ahead and get to work and compete with you after six months or whatever it is, but you get the prize for a while. We build a structure so we can share better. What's wrong with the economic structure of this world is that we're not worth a damn at sharing. We're really good at trying to protect our stash.

NDW: Of course. Out of our cultural story, out of myth number two there's not enough. If there was enough we'd change all of this but our cultural story says there's not enough.

BB: There's not enough defense, there's not enough money, not enough love.

NDW: Not enough sex.

BB: Not enough sex.

NDW: I agree on that one. (Laughter) Part of the problem here though is that this idea of "not enough-ness" is what's created the necessity to compete with each other.

If we thought there was enough, competition would no longer exist. Out of our thought that there's not enough, I think that I've got to compete with you for the stuff of which there is not enough. In our society as I observe it, Brad, is that we have decided that life is about competition because there isn't enough; there are more of us than there is the stuff we need, so I have to compete with you. The reason I have to compete with you, by the way, is because I want the stuff of which there's not enough. I want to have more than enough of that. Worse than that, the only way I can justify it because what you said at the beginning is true, is that we have an inner integrity that will not allow us just to say point blank, "Look, I'm going to take this. I'm going to take more of this than you get because I want more of this than I'm going to let you have."

We have this idea that by winning the competition, then I deserve to have this. I'll set up a system of competition that allows me to take this with impunity, to take this and feel good about taking more than you have because I'm the winner and you're the loser. I won't leave you out there with nothing but I'll have twice the share that you have because after all you're the loser and to the victor go the spoils.

BB: Or, I *will* leave you out there with nothing.

NDW: Again, because to the victor go the spoils. We're not satisfied with setting up a system of competition by which to do that. Those of us who are in positions of power on the planet have set up a competition in which we've decided ahead of time who the winners are going to be.

BB: And the winners are in a tradition that goes back to who the winners were.

NDW: That's right. I always tell my audiences I'm the big winner because I was born Roman Catholic, white, male and American. Now, you can't beat that.

BB: You got the best draw you could get.

NDW: I have four aces. Because I'm going to heaven since anyone who's not Catholic doesn't go to heaven. I'm white, so I'm going to have heaven on earth. Anyone who's not white does not have heaven on earth. I'm male, God knows that makes me better automatically, I'm sure you'd agree on that; and I'm American.

I walked into my adult life, truly, with a level of arrogance that was way beyond belief. I was raised to think that these things were true: Americans were better, maybe just a little bit better, but they were better. And Catholics were better, maybe just a little bit better, but better.

Then, from the age of twenty-one to forty-one, the world contrived to disabuse me of those notions, and one by one my illusions fell. The river of life washed away my beliefs and I finally got a boat. But in a way the beliefs I started with were necessary, as was the suffering that occurred from them, in order for me to learn how to be open to having a boat.

BB: Yes, me too. I love Pema Chödrön's perspective on this. She says, "The way we learn is through suffering. Lucky for us there's plenty of it around."

13

Organized Religion
And Traditional Belief

NDW: You know the saddest thing about organized religion to me? I don't mean to dishonor organized religion because I believe it has played a pivotal role in certain aspects of our own evolution as a species. However, I'm not sure that we could have evolved in the way that we seem to be evolving now toward a higher and grander level of experience of ourselves without organized religion.

But, having said all that . . .

BB: You have more compassion about that than I do, but go ahead.

NDW: You know why? Because it comes from my own life. I was born and raised in the Roman Catholic Church, Brad, and while that gave me a lot of baggage and I'm one of those recovering Catholics, I'm also clear that it brought me some goodies as well. Let me explain to you how I see the difference. The goodies that it brought me, is that I did grow up with a sense that there was something larger going on than just me.

I did grow up with an idea, a cosmology of some kind of a larger interactive process between All That Is and all of that. There was a larger force in the universe, call it God or whatever you want to call it, that I could rely on and call upon with dependent and consistent results. That is what the Catholic Church gave me. Compared to what I see in some kids today who grow up with no religion at all, zero, none. They have no sense of anything larger than then the baubles and bangles on their hands and toes.

I talk to the kids and I say, "Don't you have any experience of something larger?" Their experience of themselves ends at their fingertips because they've been given nothing. There's not even a bad basis or a shaky foundation. There's no foundation.

I think that the human race is better off having had the experience of organized religion than it would have been having nothing at all. The sad thing that organized religion gave us is the idea of "right" and "wrong," and "better" and "not so good." Superiority. Ironically enough, the very energy on the planet that was ostensibly designed to heal our divisions has created them and exacerbated them; not just created them but also made them worse. That's what I notice about organized religion.

Yet, having said that, it was the Catholic Church that taught me by reverse English, by not intending to, that there's no such thing as right and wrong.

Let me tell you this story because I enjoy telling about how I learned from the Roman Catholic Church that there was no such thing as right and wrong, which was exactly the opposite of what they were trying to tell me.

I was eleven years old and the first McDonalds opened in my neighborhood. I know you're old enough to remember when McDonalds didn't exit as a chain, and so am I. I remember when the first McDonalds opened in my neighborhood in Milwaukee, Wisconsin. They were giving away 500 free hamburger, French fry and Coke combinations to the first 500 people as a grand opening special. So all the kids in the neighborhood, of course, made it their business to be there.

I'm there on this morning as they open the doors and I get one of the free hamburger, French fry and Coke combinations. A bunch of kids and I were walking away and I'm eating this hamburger and I realized suddenly in the middle of this thing, "Oh, my God, it's Friday." I spit the hamburger out and the kids were saying, "What's the matter, is it that bad?" It's Friday. I forgot it was Friday.

Now, you've got to understand I was not just born and raised in the Roman Catholic Church; I was born and raised in a Catholic family on the South side of Milwaukee, Wisconsin, a heavily Polish neighborhood. It was not just Catholic, but Catholic with a capitol 'C'. I'm a very devout eleven-year-old Catholic. I'm an altar boy, if you can believe that. I'm really playing Catholic at a high level for an 11 year-old. I'm totally into the theology, I'm an altar boy and I'm studying. I imagine myself to be heading for the priesthood, and by the way, all the nuns in school said, "He has the calling."

They told me this to my face so I walked around with a crucifix tied around my neck and I thought, "I have the calling." See, now I have five reasons to be better because not only was I white, male, American and Catholic but I also had the calling. That made me even better than the other Catholics because I was going to be a priest, so I really had it made. So here I am now, this guy who's going to be a priest eating meat on Friday. I'm so upset with myself.

This is a genuine upset and I race home and run into the house and my mother looks at me and sees that I'm white as a ghost and says, "What happened? Did the kids beat you up? What happened? Are you okay?" I break into tears and say, "Yeah, I'm okay but I ate meat on Friday; I had meat. Which is a sin." And my mother held me to her chest, God bless her, and she said, "Sweetheart, honey, I'm sure that God understands. It's okay. It's all right."

She was such a lovely woman that she didn't have the heart to tell me at the age of eleven that God simply didn't give a damn. Well, maybe she didn't know. Maybe she actually thought that God cared. I didn't get that piece of information.

I went to Catechism class a few days later. The priest taught the class (and this is how I learned there's no such thing as "right" and "wrong"— I'm telling you a true story now) and at the end of his lesson he said, "Are there any other questions on this or any other subject?" which was he said at the end of every one of his lessons.

And I raised my little eleven-year-old hand and said, "Father, is it true that if you eat meat on Friday and you don't go to confession on Saturday and you get hit by a car on Sunday and die, on Monday you're in Hell?" (Laughter)

The priest said, "Oh no, that's a misconception, son. That's not true. You'd be in purgatory."

I said, "Well, what is purgatory?"

"Well, purgatory is the same as hell but it's not forever."

I had a couple of marriages like that, Brad. (Laughter) I'm just kidding!

So I sat there and he described purgatory to me. He said, "Purgatory is the place where your sins get burned off your soul and that's only if you have venial sins. If you have mortal sins, do not pass 'Go,' do not collect $200; you go straight to hell if you should die with an unconfessed mortal sin on your soul. If you have confessed that mortal sin, or if you just have venial sin, then you go to purgatory and it gets burned off."

So I said, "How long do you stay in purgatory?"

"That depends on how many sins you've committed," he said.

So there's a system of divine justice that takes place and you get sentenced to a certain number of years in purgatory. Now, the sisters told us in school that if you have someone on earth praying for you, that can reduce your sentence. They would say to us kids, "Pray for the poor departed souls in purgatory." We would actually do that. I would actually go to the church and earnestly pray to God, pray for the dear departed soul of my Grandma. This is sad, because I'm praying for my Grandmother who I thought was an angel anyway. But I'm assured that she had enough sins that she wouldn't go straight to heaven. She'd spend some weeks, months, minutes, whatever, in purgatory.

There I was at eleven years old sitting there saying, "God, please, let Grandma out."

Now, you think I'm making this up, but this is how it was, you see? Part of me knew this couldn't be true. This is how I learned there is no "right" and "wrong," by explaining this. At the age of eleven, I thought, "Wait a minute. God can't be this insane. We're talking about an insane God here."

At eleven I saw the insanity of that. So I'm thinking now, "Okay, how can I get this priest to see what I see?" So I decided to ask pin-him-in-the-corner questions.

I said, "Father, what about if a little baby were to die just after birth? Surely that baby would go straight to Our Father Who's in Heaven without having to stop in purgatory or anyplace else."

The priest said, "No, not if it wasn't baptized. If the baby wasn't baptized it would not go to heaven."

I said, "A two-hour-old infant who couldn't do anything wrong to offend God? Where would it go, to hell?"

"Oh, no, no no. It wouldn't go to hell, son."

"To purgatory?"

"No, it wouldn't go to purgatory."

"Well, where would it go?"

"Limbo."

I said, "Limbo? What is limbo?"

Now my mind is really going crazy and I'm clear that this guy is a very mixed-up person, but he looks like Bing Crosby in "Going My Way" and he has a little white slit there in the collar. I think that I can't challenge his authority any further; I've pushed him as far as I can push him. So, at age eleven and because I wanted to stay an altar boy in that church and didn't want to offend the authority, I let it go.

For the remaining years, that burned in me because I knew that that couldn't be the way it is. It can't be like that. God does not say to a two-hour-old infant, "Sorry, your parents didn't baptize you so it's a tough break but that's just how it is up here."

Now, I'm twenty-one years old. It's ten years later and at the age of twenty-one I pick up the newspaper. In the "Milwaukee Journal" religion section I read, "The Pope declares eating meat on Friday no longer a sin." I'm thinking, "Now, let me see if I got this right. The Pope has now come to the conclusion that I came to at eleven. Okay." I wanted desperately to find that priest. I even went back to the parish to see if he was there but he wasn't there any more. I couldn't find him. I had this imaginary conversation with the priest. I fantasized that one day I'd run into him and say:

"Father! Father, have you heard the news?"

"Yes, my son."

"Does that mean if I have meat this Friday and I don't go to confession on Saturday and I get hit by a car on Sunday and die, on Monday I won't be in purgatory?"

"That's right, my son."

"But if I had meat last Friday . . . ?"

I couldn't help but wonder, what does God say to all those thousands of people who had all those millions of McDonalds hamburgers on Friday? "It seemed like a good idea at the time"?

I'm not making fun of the Roman Catholic Church because the truth is, I could make up these stories about any religion on the face of the earth.

BB: Absolutely. I make fun of all of them. I'm an equal opportunity wise-cracker about hypocrisy.

NDW: We have to be able to laugh at ourselves. It isn't about ridicule, it's about seeing how we've constructed it and then looking back over our shoulder and saying isn't it funny that we actually allowed ourselves to believe that? Not to ridicule anyone but I do like to point out to people in hopefully a mildly humorous way, "Look folks, we're making it all up. We're making it all up, and we're just creating it that way. Right and wrong are just figments of our imagination."

Yet, this is not an argument for abandoning our system of right and wrong, it's an argument for continuing to create it because we are the product of our choices and decisions. Every act is an act of self definition and we're defining ourselves; we're recreating ourselves anew in every single moment of now and we have to use these devices that we call "right and wrong" or "what works and what doesn't work," whatever the label.

We have to use these devices to know ourselves in every moment. When we start taking it so seriously, and when we aren't clear that we're making it all up but we think that someone else, some Higher Power, is making it all up which then gives us the power to shoot each other when we don't agree. That's when organized religion becomes (as it always has been, of course) dangerous to our health.

We should have a stamp on every church bulletin in the world like they do on cigarettes, you know: "This Church is hazardous to your health," so that you know what you're getting into. Having said that, Brad, I want to make it clear that I still think organized religions do have some good things to offer. They offer a sense of reverence for life, a sense of awareness that there's something larger than our own individual experience and our own selves, and a sense of communion with All That Is. These are among the best of the religious teachings among the best of the religions. But boy, we've got to get rid of some of that trash.

14

About the Spirit,

And How Institutions Change

Brad started out as a member of the Christian Faith and Life Community thirty years ago and did extracurricular study in Theology. He was a preacher in the Methodist church. When he was twenty years old, he was a circuit preacher with three churches in Texas. His fundamental grounding is in existentialist theology and in Buddhism. Christian existentialism was the first shining of the light to him that had something to do with demythologizing the Church and getting over the adolescent view that, if he was just good enough, he would earn enough credits to get into Heaven. (Fortunately, both of us had to give up on that. And lucky for us that we did.)

That existentialist theological perspective is what shows up in Brad's distinction of what he calls *mind* and *being*.

•••

BB: Your fundamental identity and my fundamental identity right now is this: I am a person sitting in a chair talking to you and listening to you, and you're a person sitting in a chair talking to me and listening. That's who you are and this is who I am. *This current experience is my primary identity.* My case history and the records of my mind, the culture I grew up in, the belief systems that I have, are all secondary. Once we shift that figure and ground so that our true identity, *the noticing being in the moment* comes forward, then the self-image identity, the identification with our case history, recedes to the background. It's as though all the worry of the mind meets the presence of the being—that's what I call what you designate as God's voice in your books— which comes forward as who you are. All the stuff that's your case history, and your story about your-self, recedes to the background. What happened to you in your life is still true, but it's secondary to your primary identity. Who you *actually* are is a being that notices moment to moment to moment. Who you are, is a *being* sitting in a chair looking at me listening, and I'm a *being* talking and looking at you. If we hold that as fundamentally who I am and fundamentally who you are, who you are as a personality is secondary and who I am as a personality is secondary. I can honor the being that you are by just being the being that I am. I don't have to do anything!

NDW: You're not a human-doing; you're a human being.

BB: Yes! Actually we're both. We do, in fact, do things a lot. But we have to get our priorities straight. Once we just acknowledge that each other's being is our *primary* identity then we *beings* can *use our minds* and do things. The whole question about society is: Are the minds in service to *being* or is *being* in service to the mind? In individual lives, when the being is in service to the mind, everything goes wrong because the mind becomes a bunch of principles and attached values and a whole bunch of shoulds and rights and wrongs. The mind is just a terrible, terrible, terrible master because it makes such overriding generaliza-tions and forces you to be obedient to them in order to be who you are in your mind.

NDW: We've got to stop "shoulding" on ourselves.

BB: Ain't it the truth! The best way to me to honor the being of another human being is to be completely transparent, completely open and completely honest. That's how I honor the being that you are. I just tell you the truth. It doesn't matter if I've got judgments about you being a jerk or not, that's just a part of my judgments. We think opinions are so important. Opinions aren't important at all! We generate opinions just like we make feces. We eat perfectly good food and turn it into feces. We take perfectly good experience and turn it into opinions. That's the analogy. I don't much care what your opinion is of me, or my opinion of you except when I do. Then, if I do, I'll tell you about it and get over it. Opinions don't count for much. It's the honoring of all Being by the being I am, being present to your being and you being present to me in the same way.

If people work from a place of honoring the being of their own being and the being of other human beings and use their minds in obedience to that connection, then *they can't go wrong.* They'll come up with wonderful creative solutions and they'll take care of each other. But when they come from their minds about the way they "should" behave and all Being is secondary to the goals and values and judgments of the mind, then *they'll always go wrong.* The problem is that we keep going back, falling back into our own minds, *we keep mistakenly identifying ourselves as our minds.* However, if we recover often, through conscious practices like meditation and radical honesty with each other, we can frequently *reclaim our identity as beings.* So at least it ends up being a shared-time experience with the being in charge of the mind sometimes, and then the mind being in charge of being again, until we recover our being again, and so on. (So we find our mind leading, then we find our true selves again and for a little while *being* is leading, then the mind takes over again and for a while is leading, then the being leading again, etc.) This is why Sartre finally said, "You cannot separate your being and your doing." Since Sartre said that, we have discovered that, although it is true that we cannot separate our being and our doing, we can remind ourselves and each other constantly to *surrender* to being so we don't *stay* lost in mind land. That is why Frank Sinatra became the greatest philosopher of the 20th century because he said, "do-be-do-be-do." (Laughter)

I'm also hopeful, because I think that gradually, gradually, through the work that a lot of people are doing, including our work, people are coming to honor being over mind. That's why I am committed to the vision of a possible world for future human beings, where every human being born on the planet can have the possibility of a lifetime of play and service to other human beings, instead of a lifetime of neurotic defense of self-image, competition, greed and warfare.

NDW: How many people do you think actually understand what you just said out of the average hundred people in a room? Out of a hundred people in any room, how many people do you think would have followed what you just said and understood it enough to say, "That is a solution; that is an answer; I get that."?

BB: Two.

NDW: I was wondering what your answer would be. My next question behind that is, how can we get the other ninety-eight?

BB: We've got to keep talking. We just have to keep talking.

NDW: You know, the Pope just made an interesting declaration—just as a follow-up to close that loop. On the 28th of July, 1999 Pope Paul II held an audience.

At that time he was in very bad health and looking at the possibility of his own mortality, of his own death, and he went off to the Papal retreat in the mountains of Italy. Three weeks later, he came back and held an audience. In his audience he delivered a homily, in which he essentially said that there's no such place as hell. He told his audience, and I am paraphrasing here, that people must be very careful in interpreting the biblical descriptions of hell, which he said are merely symbolic and metaphorical. Hell as a place of fire and brimstone is a figment of our imagination and a product of our mythologies.

There is an experience called "hell," which I believe to be separation from God, and hence from each other. That's a hell-like experience. The

Pope agrees, saying that hell is more than a place, rather, "it is the situation in which one finds himself after freely and definitively withdrawing from God, the source of life and joy."

He also said that this experience of hell is not something that God visits upon you. It "is not a punishment inflicted by God from outside," the Pope declared. "Rather, it is the further, final development of a denial of God which a person begins on earth." In other words, God is not a punishing, retributive, vengeful deity. We bring our own personal experience of hell upon ourselves.

And finally—now get *this*—the pope said he wasn't even sure if anyone was actually in hell. That, he said, "remains a real possibility, but is not something we can know."

That's the Pope talking now, quoted directly. Have you ever heard any Christian teacher, much less the *Pope,* declare that whether souls are in hell is not something they can know? Until now, everyone's been very *certain* about this! This is what they've used to *scare us.* Now here's John Paul II saying we can't even be sure that *anyone* is *in* hell!

BB: The Pope has been reading "Conversations with God"!

NDW: You just stole my punch line. (Laughter) That's right. That's the conclusion I came to. Somebody said, in fact, that the Pope had been reading the Trilogy.

Now unless you were a Catholic for most of your life, you wouldn't understand how earth-shaking that last statement was, because not even a Catholic priest at the parish level, much less the Pope, would ever say in my lifetime, "We can't be sure" that anyone is in hell.

Believe me, when I was young they were deathly sure that there were souls in hell, and their absolute assurance that there were souls in hell was the entire basis of their fear-based theology. "There's no question that there are souls in hell and I'll tell you how you're going to get there. If you keep bugging me in class like this, kid . . ." It was like that.

Now here's the Pope saying these extraordinary things. And you're right, Brad. The fact is that these same statements were made in "Conversations with God." It's either a coincidence or it's not. I have heard that someone slipped him a copy of the Trilogy. I don't want to be arrogant enough to assume that something that came through me has changed the whole theology of the whole Roman Catholic Church, but I do think that there's a shift in consciousness on the planet. To which you are adding, I am adding, and Marianne Williamson, James Redfield, Deepak Chopra, Gary Zukav, Jean Houston, Barbara Marx Hubbard, and many others not mentioned here, are adding—including some theologians within the various churches and religions.

I think that there's this awakening that's taking place and this awakening is filtering not just downward but upward and people like the Pope are taking a long, hard look at it and saying, "You know, maybe there's another interpretation. Maybe there's another way." They're broadening our base of understanding and gradually moving away from fear-based theologies.

To me, for the Pope to make those statements was remarkable. However, equally remarkable and perhaps more so was that the international press, the worldwide press, gave it practically no attention.

BB: That *is* unbelievable. I know how remarkable that is, not from having been a Catholic, but from having seen so many of them.

NDW: Talk about an eight-column headline statement, but that didn't make the headlines. It was in the press all right, but on page thirty-six in the lower left-hand corner. I saw that and I contacted the Catholic News Service to make sure that I hadn't misread it or that the paper hadn't misreported it. No, he said those things. So, I think now all that has to happen is for the establishment, for the power structure of the world to get it. This statement by the Pope really rattles the power structure not just of the Roman Catholic Church, but also of the world. Our belief in these fearful things has been driving the engine of our experience all along and pushing us away from telling the truth to each other and being authentic with each other and simply being with each other.

There's a fabulous movie out called "Instinct."

BB: I've heard of it, but I haven't seen it.

NDW: Fabulous movie! The main character grabbed his would-be lawyer around the neck and asked him, "What have you just now lost? If you tell me what you lost, I will let you go." Now, he's got him by the neck and the guy can hardly talk but he gives him a crayon to write with and the guy writes "Control." He says, "No, you idiot!" and tightens his grip on his throat and asks, "What have you lost?"

"Freedom."

"NO!"

After several attempts, he says, "Okay, I'll give you one last chance and then I'll have to break your neck. What have you lost? Think!"

The guy writes, "My illusions," and he lets the guy go.

BB: AH! Very good.

NDW: He tells him, "That is correct. You never did have control, just the illusion of it. Now I've cracked your illusion, and now I can let you go."

BB: See, that's all we've got to do! Just get everybody around the neck like this and ask, "So what have you lost??" (Laughter)

NDW: That's the solution right there. Sometimes you have to do that with people, figuratively. You've got to grab them by the scruff of the neck and say, "Wake up! Wake up and see what's so!"

BB: Marianne Williamson, at the end of "Healing the Soul of America," said what I later paraphrased in my testimony when I was arrested and went to trial. She was the author who talked about the world as a village of one hundred people, which I mentioned in my article quoted on page 110.

I think about Marianne Williamson's analogy a lot. If we were in a village of a hundred people and we all knew these facts about each other, if we could see and smell and hear each other, it would have an effect on the consciousness of everyone in the room. If we could actually have an experience of what it's like to not have good shelter when it's cold and windy or raining at night, or in the intense heat of the day, or

what it's like to be malnourished so you're sick a lot and more suscep-
tible to disease all the time, and not be very clean because you don't
have sanitation—to experience the ongoing fear of losing a loved one,
possibly tomorrow, or losing your own life on short notice. If we were
there together, and we were all talking, we'd discover that six people in
that village would control enough of the resources available to essentially control everyone in the room—and all six of those people would be
citizens of the United States of America.

If we could be aware of the way things are in a group of one hundred people, I really believe that we would work it out. I believe we
would all eventually say, "Look, I'll go ahead and buy your supper tonight, or let's get to work and fix up these houses so that people don't
have to be exposed to the wind and rain all the time. Let's give these kids
some water and food, then figure out some way where people can go
defecate somewhere other than in the camp. Let's get some water and
fix this up. You guys who have got money, instead of hiring those six
other guys with sub-machine guns to guard your corner of the room,
just give up one hireling and one sub-machine gun and we'll use that
money to do this work of fixing up the houses and buying some seed
and getting some clean water and medicine, okay?"

Out of the conversation that would occur in that group of a hundred people, honestly sharing how their lives really are, a solution would
come that was compassionate. *But we haven't figured out how to do it
on a large enough scale that allows all of us to be compassionate, and
have it show up in the way we are actually organized to treat each other.*
Fifty percent of the world's population is malnourished. The problem is,
with six billion of us on the planet, we have this hard time being compassionate on the scale required. *Three hundred and eighty five families
control more of the world's resources than the lower half of the nations
of the world.* That's the way things are, actually, in the world right now.
The question is how can we be compassionate on a larger scale?

NDW: Well, I think what you're talking about, Brad, is a decision
that we have to make ourselves as a human race. What you're driving at,
what you're discussing, as I'm experiencing it, is the basic nature of humans:

the basic nature of the human being. In "Conversations With God," I was told that the most crucial decision the human race will make in the twenty-first century, and it will come sooner rather than later, probably in the next ten or twenty years, has to do with how we imagine ourselves with regard to our basic nature. Are we basically good or are we at our basis, evil? To put that into the terms you just described, if we were in that room with a hundred people, would those six people, having seen the problem and how easy and within their own capabilities it is to solve, would they? That's part of the problem because we don't think we can solve it. We don't think we're capable. If we were six out of a hundred, we'd say, "We can solve this. You put in twenty, I'll put in twenty, someone else put in twenty and we'll solve this." But would we? That's the basic decision we have to make.

As I was told in the "Conversations," right now, we as a society, have made a decision that we wouldn't. That is the understanding of the largest number of people. It's our cultural story that starts off with our being born in original sin and all that. It's our cultural story and our basis that, left to our own devices, we would do the evil thing, or the thing that serves only us, the self-serving thing. Therefore, in the room of a hundred people those six people would not do what you suggest.

BB: The thing is that *what is self-serving turns out to be compassion.*

NDW: Of course, if you expand your definition of self-interest.

BB: What I'm saying is that human beings will *see.* Yes. I'm professing a faith in human beings, I realize that. My view of the nature of human beings is a "both/and" rather than an "either/or." Human beings, if you go down to the sub-scale of good and evil, are both good and evil. What they are, basically, is selfish and compassionate. If I look at you and see another Holy Human Prototype, like I was talking about before, and you see a Holy Human Prototype here, and we both get that, *I can generate the Golden Rule out of my experience of being in contact with you.* Of course I'm going to treat you the way I'd want to be treated, because you and I are alike so much that it's just natural for me to have compassion. If you say, "I'm hurting," I think, "Well, where are you hurting?" You tell me. "I feel a little pain there." I might say, "I'm sorry. What can I do to help?" There's some kind of way that that comes out of people. I swear it comes out of people. It comes out of the meanest people. It doesn't matter how mean they are, if they've killed people or anything else, it still comes out of them.

I believe that is basically our nature. It's also our nature to be very aggressive and violent and competitive on the basis of not only taking stuff away from other people but our basic appetites. We want to eat when we want to eat. We want to have sex when we want to have sex, that's a given. At the same time, if all those things are turned on at once (that is, you have the lust and you have the greed and all that stuff and you also have the connection with other people), and you *acknowledge everything and tell the truth about it, what works out between people is that they work out a way that everybody gets almost everything they want.* They can do that. We know that we can do that by relating to each other as one being to another. What gets in the way is our mind— the stories we are living in.

Our cultural story, I agree, is a way that we agree to think about things. A culture is, actually, attachment to a bunch of beliefs. Fundamentally when you're dumped into a culture you become attached to the beliefs of that culture. You sustain the culture by maintaining the belief system. Now, as you say, we've gotten to this place where we have to re-do the belief system of society so it includes every human being, not just little groups of people fighting with each other over who gets to keep what. One of the things we have to do before we do that is to acknowledge the truth about human beings. That is: *human beings have appetites and human beings also have the ability to identify with each other.* Both are true. It's not one or the other, it's both, and given that, and having that kind of perspective on what a human being is, why can't we just work out how to get it together? It's okay with me if you're selfish or if you're hungry and you want to eat. I understand that. I'm that way, too.

NDW: That's the trick of course, our appetites are identical. I don't want anything that you don't want. Once I get that, and once I get that because you identify with me you're not going to take my stuff in order to get what you want, that's crucial.

BB: Then we can cooperate.

NDW: Then we can cooperate and both of us can go out and get it over there; we don't have to get it from each other.

BB: Or, we can get it from each other but we can figure out a way to do it so we don't rip each other off.

NDW: Do it in a way that works, yeah. Gosh. That's a wonderful construction, a wonderful verbal construction. I'm just wondering how we get from where we are to where we want to be; how we get from the way we now are interacting to that place you're now discussing.

BB: I think the way we get there is through a conversation, like this one, that we just keep going. We have this conversation. People hear this conversation; they have a conversation about this conversation. You continue this conversation in your presentations and in your writing and I continue it in my presentations and my writing. There are lots of other people that are engaged at different levels of this conversation, other authors and speakers and people who are rising in business.
You know Ben Cohen, business executive of Ben and Jerry's Ice Cream fame, is in on this conversation and is making a political move about it. He's saying, "Let's reduce the Pentagon spending budget by 15% and give it to kids." It's a good idea. There are lots of generals and former chiefs-of-staff and lots of business executives that are in the group with him called Businessmen for Sensible Priorities. He believes in the possibility that we can actually control our resources democratically, according to what we know people really want. If we simply say "Look, we could take this Pentagon money and spend it on schools and children. Don't you want to do that?" Most people already want that but the control of the votes is with the multi-national corporations, whose vested selfish

interests are to keep the military industrial complex going, even though the Cold War has been over for ten years. But if politicians and business-men can get this, anyone can. Even politicians can get it eventually. At least Ben Cohen thinks that even politicians could get it.

You know, one of the things that teaches people to live in their minds and not their bodies is a law school education. Most of our politi-cians are lawyers, so we have to be very, very compassionate about politi-cians because they're usually the la-a-a-ast one to "get it." It takes a lot of love to put up with a politician. It's like trying to love a lawyer. (Laughter)

You know, three hundred years ago Kierkegaard said, "A person who relates to another person and relates also to that relation, relates thereby to God." What he meant, I think, was this: that the way we are able to relate to all of Being is by one being relating to another being and being consciously aware of that relating.

Spirituality has always, always been about Being rather than prin-ciple or ideal or holding up God's image, or any of those things. It's always been about the nourishment of relatedness and presence to each other that comes through noticing and contact. It's never really been about whose theology can whip someone else's theology, or who's right and who's wrong. Those arguments were all after the fact of the occur-rence of true spirit.

The religious experience is an experience of contact. People always ask me "Do you believe in God? " and I say, "No. I don't believe in God. I have an experience of God." And that's the way I talk about it. The way that I have an experience of God is by being in contact with you while I'm present to my own being.

NDW: In answer to the question, "Do you believe in God?" I also say, "No, I don't believe in God. I *know,* and knowing is not believing, knowing is knowing. I give the same answer that you do, ultimately. They say, "Well, how do you know?" and I say, "Well, because I'm talk-ing with you."

BB: Right!

NDW: I think it comes down really to the same thing. You know, I think it's remarkable that you and I should have such common ground. We've never, ever had a conversation like this. I bet some people reading or hearing us right now might think that we've been friends for years or known each other for twenty-five years, but this is really the first time I've ever talked with you.

BB: I know, we really rehearsed this well, didn't we? (Laughter)

NDW: I'm fascinated by how much common ground we hold, out of a simple chance meeting on an airplane. But you know, I read your book. I didn't really read "Radical Honesty." I lied about that, but I read portions of it, a chapter here and a chapter there. More importantly, what was happening in my life was that everywhere I went, people were holding the book up when I would finish my lecture and say, "Have you read 'Radical Honesty'?" Finally, after the fiftieth person said, "Have you read 'Radical Honesty'?" I thought, "Enough already! What does he do, send people around to my lectures?" After I read a few chapters I thought, "This son-of-a-gun has stolen my material!"

BB: That's what I thought when I read "Conversations with God." You robbed me and Werner; what were you doing? (Laughter)

NDW: I've got that question, too. I got a nice letter from Werner a while ago honoring the courage that he saw it took to put this message out there, and he said he wanted to acknowledge that it had been done with such accessibility and clarity. That was a nice letter to get from Werner Erhard, whose mind, I think, is brilliant. A brilliant mind.

BB: Me, too. I think so, too.

NDW: But here we are, and then I met you on an airplane. There you are, walking down the aisle, and I'm thinking, "My God, it's Brad Blanton!"

BB: I know! I almost believe in divine intervention, because I missed a plane at Dulles airport in Washington and went screaming back down to the Charlottesville airport to make it to the talk I had to give that night in Florida. I just jumped on the first plane that was available. I got there just past the time the plane was supposed to take off. It was a little delayed, so I got on it. It almost makes me believe in divine intervention! Of course, I don't believe in that. (Laughter)

NDW: Well, *I do!* Because you're here! It's the evidence of my life that upholds a system of divine intervention. (Laughter)

BB: If we keep on this conversation, before long we'll have a Catholic Church again. (Laughter)

NDW: It's the last thing we need here.

BB: I sure have enjoyed the hell out of this conversation.

NDW: I've enjoyed the hell out of it too, enjoyed the hell right out of it! Whew! That's what we need to do in our lives, enjoy "the hell" out of it.

BB: Okay, that'll be our motto, "Enjoy the hell out of it."

NDW: It's exciting to be talking with you, Brad. I've got to tell you straight up, you have got one of the most brilliant minds I've engaged in a very long time.

BB: Thank you. I really liked this conversation with you, too. It's been great. I'd like to keep the conversation going.

NDW: Let's do that.

BB: All right. I think the conversation between us is a conversation that in a way is just representative of a conversation that's going on among literally millions of people. We're not the only ones talking about this. What gives me more inspiration than anything else is that I know that we're not the only ones talking about this. The reason people are listening to us is because we're saying things they already know to be true and have actually begun talking about. People get really excited when we do these presentations, and we talk to them afterwards. You know how people don't want to go away at the end of a meeting? It's because they don't want to leave when it feels like they are in contact with other human beings talking about the way life really is. People are in love with the truth.

NDW: Amen!

PART IV

Honest to God Together

15

September 11, 2001

When we sat down to write this book, we had no idea how timely the material would turn out to be. We knew how profoundly appropriate it was in the history of the human experience, to now confront at the next highest level, the whole subject of radical honesty, but we couldn't have guessed how important it would be in terms of the acuteness of its timing. We write this last section of this book, essentially as a postscript in the aftermath of the September 11th events and the events which have followed that. Now we are clearer than ever, that unless we can move into the experience of radical honesty, of total transparency and complete vulnerability with each other, there may soon be nothing to be honest, transparent and vulnerable about.

We are now discussing the very future of the human species, the survival of Homo sapiens; the next outcome could be the last. So, everything that you've read in this book up to now, we're sure you've already read in a new context, since this book was published after those events. But we wanted you to know that the words that follow here were written after those events.

If there was ever a time in which the rubber meets the road, it's now. Soon after the events of September 11, 2001, both Brad and Neale wrote letters to their readers, workshop graduates and friends. When we each read what the other had to say, we found that we not only liked what we read but were very much struck by the applicability of our just-completed manuscript to the problem of terrorism and anti-terrorism. We then felt that, more than ever, we had to do what we could to contribute to the creation of a new model for how we human beings organize ourselves to live together. We both know, as do a number of our colleagues in spirit, that we now, more than ever, have to come up with some way that allows us groups of human beings to not be constantly trying to destroy each other.

So, after reading what each other wrote about the events, we quickly arranged another dialogue because we wanted to focus our energies on the matters that are before the human family right now as they have never been in the past. We met in Virginia Beach, where Brad attended Neale's presentation there on a Wednesday night, and on Thursday morning we taped our conversation and have made it into this final section of "Honest to God"

This is the truly applied part. This is about what we both consider to be the critical issue of our time, namely the need for spiritual leadership based on honesty and on knowing that we are all one. So this special addition to complete the manuscript of "Honest to God" is devoted to the exploration of numerous options for the transformation of the world in the wake of the September 11th call to action. The question is: What kind of action?

What follows here in Chapter 16 is material written by Neale just hours after the tragedy. Then, Chapter 17 is a slightly modified version of Brad's article soon thereafter, and quotes from friends. Chapters 18, 19 and 20 are from the edited transcript of our dialogue with each other about the events. What we have talked and written about, with each other's help, is what actions all of us might take to actually bring about an end to terrorism and the creation of a new future.

In light of the recent events, you can't help but notice how extraordinarily relevant this conversation you are about to read is—especially with regard to the co-creation of our common future. If you take what you read here into your lives, together we can write a new chapter in the history of the human race. Each one of us human beings who are aware of this conversation is a leader and a model for other human beings. Please read this as a call to action.

16

Letter from Neale

A few hours after the first terrorist attacks on the World Trade Center in New York City and the Pentagon in Washington D.C., Neale posted the following statement at conversationswithgod.org, his official website. The statement was picked up by the media and by Internet watchers, and within hours had been sent across the globe.

•••

September 11, 2001

Dear friends around the world . . .

The events of this day cause every thinking person to stop their daily lives, whatever is going on in them, and to ponder deeply the larger questions of life. We search again for not only the meaning of life, but the purpose of our individual and collective experience as we have created it—and we look earnestly for ways in which we might recreate ourselves anew as a human species, so that we will never treat each other this way again.

The hour has come for us to demonstrate at the highest level our most extraordinary thought about Who We Really Are.

There are two possible responses to what has occurred today. The first comes from love, the second from fear.

If we come from fear we may panic and do things—as individuals and as nations—that could only cause further damage. If we come from love we will find refuge and strength, even as we provide it to others.

A central teaching of "Conversations with God" is: What you wish to experience, provide for another.

Look to see, now, what it is you wish to experience—in your own life, and in the world. Then see if there is another for whom you may be the source of that.

If you wish to experience peace, provide peace for another.

If you wish to know that you are safe, cause another to know that they are safe.

If you wish to better understand seemingly incomprehensible things, help another to better understand.

If you wish to heal your own sadness or anger, seek to heal the sadness or anger of another.

If you wish to have justice done, you are invited to act justly with all others.

Those others are waiting for you now. They are looking to you for guidance, for help, for courage, for strength, for understanding, and for assurance at this hour. Most of all, they are looking to you for love.

This is the moment of your ministry. This is the time of teaching. What you teach at this time, through your every word and action right now, will remain as indelible lessons in the hearts and minds of those whose lives you touch, both now, and for years to come.

We will set the course for tomorrow, today. At this hour. In this moment.

There is much we can do, but there is one thing we cannot do. We cannot continue to co-create our lives together on this planet as we have in the past. We cannot, except at our peril, ignore the events of this day, or their implications.

It is tempting at times like this to give in to rage. Anger is fear announced, and rage is anger that is repressed which, when it is released, is often misdirected. Right now, anger is not inappropriate. It is, in fact, natural—and can be a blessing. If we use our anger about this day, not to pinpoint where the blame falls, but where the cause lies, we can lead the way to healing.

Let us seek not to pinpoint blame, but to pinpoint cause.

Unless we take this time to look at the cause of our experience, we will never remove ourselves from the experiences it creates. Instead, we will forever live in fear of retribution from those within the human family who feel aggrieved, and, likewise, seek retribution from them.

So at this time it is important for us to direct our anger toward the cause of our present experience. And that is not only individuals or groups who have attacked others, but also the reasons they have done so. Unless we look at these reasons, we will never be able to eliminate these attacks.

To me the reasons are clear. We have not learned the most basic human lessons. We have not remembered the most basic human truths. We have not understood the most basic spiritual wisdom. In short, we have not been listening to God, and because we have not, we watch ourselves do ungodly things.

The message of "Conversations with God" is clear: we are all one. That is a message the human race has largely ignored. Our separation mentality has underscored all of our human creations.

Our religions, our political structures, our economic systems, our educational institutions, and our whole approach to life, have been based on the idea that we are separate from each other. This has caused us to inflict all manner of injury, one upon the other. And this injury causes other injury, for like begets like and negativity only breeds negativity.

It is as easy to understand as that. And so now let us pray that all of us in this human family will find the courage and the strength to turn inward and to ask a simple, soaring question: what would love do now?

If we could love even those who have attacked us, and seek to understand why they have done so, what then would be our response? Yet if we meet negativity with negativity, rage with rage, attack with attack, what then will be the outcome?

These are the questions that are placed before the human race today. They are questions that we have failed to answer for thousands of years. Failure to answer them now could eliminate the need to answer them at all.

We should make no mistake about this. The human race has the power to annihilate itself. We can end life as we know it on this planet in one afternoon.

This is the first time in human history that we have been able to say this. And so now we must direct our attention to the questions that such power places before us. And we must answer these questions from a spiritual perspective, not a political perspective, and not an economic perspective.

We must have our own conversation with God, for only the grandest wisdom and the grandest truth can address the greatest problems, and we are now facing the greatest problems and the greatest challenges in the history of our species.

If we want the beauty of the world that we have co-created to be experienced by our children and our children's children, we will have to become spiritual activists right here, right now, and cause that to happen. We must choose to be at cause in the matter.

So, talk with God today. Ask God for help, for counsel and advice, for insight and for strength and for inner peace and for deep wisdom. Ask God on this day to show us how to show up in the world in a way that will cause the world itself to change.

That is the challenge that is placed before every thinking person today. Today the human soul asks the question: What can I do to preserve the beauty and the wonder of our world and to eliminate the anger and hatred——and the disparity that inevitably causes it——in that part of the world which I touch?

Please seek to answer that question today, with all the magnificence that is You.

I love you, and I send you my deepest thoughts of peace.

Neale Donald Walsch

• • •

Since the posting of that statement Neale has been asked by the press and by people throughout the world to expand on his thoughts. These additional comments have appeared in newspapers and in magazine articles:

There is a familiar song which contains words that were never, ever more meaningful than they are today:

What the world needs now is love, sweet love. That's the only thing that there's just too little of. What the world needs now is love, sweet love. No, not just for some, but for everyone.

I have said over and over again in this country and in talks throughout the world, that all of our problems, all of our turmoil, all of our tendencies to hurt and to harm each other would be eliminated, disappeared, literally wiped out of our experience, if we but accepted the message which has been given us again in "Conversations with God" that We Are All One.

The Bible, which is only one of humanity's many sources of spiritual teaching, carries this message throughout, in both the Old and New Testaments.

It appears in Malachi 2:10, as *"Have we not all one father? Has not one God created us? Why then are we faithless to one another, profaning the covenant of our fathers?"*

It appears in Romans 12:5, where it is written, *"So we, though many, are one body in Christ, and individually members one of another."*

It appears in 1 Corinthians 10:17 . . . *"Because there is one bread, we who are many are one body."*

Over and over we have been taught this. All of our faith traditions bring us this truth. Yet we cannot and will not accept it and act as if it were true. There seems to be one thing for which many human beings will give up anything. They will give up peace, love, happiness, joy, prosperity, romance, excitement, serenity, *everything*—even their own health—for this one thing:

Being right.

But even if we *are* right, even if we think that everything we are doing to each other on this planet is justified by our grievances, what is spirituality's recommended course of action? What do the greatest spiritual teachers of all time, each in their own way, tell us at times such as these? It is something that many of us cannot seem, or simply do not *wish,* to hear.

"I say unto you, *love* your enemies, *bless* them that curse you, *do good* to them that hate you, and pray for them that despitefully use you and persecute you."

Can this be sound advice?

This much I know. It is easy at times like this to mistake rage for justice. Yet rage never produces authentic justice. Indeed, it inevitably creates *injustice*—for someone. That is because rage is anger that has been repressed, and, when released, it is always misdirected. *This is exactly what happened on September 11, 2001.*

In the early days of our civilization, we were able to express our rage and inflict hurt upon each other by using sticks and rocks and primitive weapons. Then, as our technology grew, we could destroy a village, or a town, or a major city, or even an entire nation. Yet, as I continue to note, now it is possible for us to destroy our whole world, and do it so fast that nothing can stop the process once it has begun.

Is that the process we wish to begin? This is the question we must answer.

It should be no surprise that we are facing this question now. It is not as if we have not seen this coming. Spiritual, political, and philosophical writers for the past 50 years have predicted it. So long as we continue to treat each other as we have in the past, they have said, the circumstance we face in the present will continue to present itself in the future.

We must change ourselves. We must change the beliefs upon which our behaviors are based. We must create a different reality, build a new society. And we must do so not with political truths or with economic truths, and not with cultural truths or even the remembered truths of our ancestors—for the sins of the fathers are being visited upon the sons. We must do so with new spiritual truths. We must preach a new gospel, its healing message summarized in two sentences:

We are all one.

Ours is not a better way, ours is merely another way.

This fifteen-word message, delivered from every lectern and pulpit, from every rostrum and platform, in every mosque, church and temple, could change the world overnight. I challenge every priest, every imam, every minister, and every rabbi to preach this. I challenge every political party spokesperson and the head of every national government to de-clare it.

And I challenge all of us, right now, to become spiritual activists. If we want the beauty of the world and not its ugliness to be experienced by our children and our children's children, *we must choose to be at cause in the matter.*

17

Some Sorrow in Samsara

By Brad Blanton

Through communications on the Internet many of us have had the chance to overcome some of the limitations of perspective of the general commentary on TV and radio. There *is* a conversation to be engaged in that is something other than the usual infantile perspective our government and the commentators in the media have had to offer so far.

The conversation has begun about what we can do in the changed world after the suicide bombings of the Pentagon and the World Trade Center, but the really important questions are not publicly delved into except by individuals who are not afraid of being seen as unpatriotic rather than corporate entities.

Even National Public Radio and CNN and PBS have not really talked about why the terrorists might want to do such a thing. The President's answer to that question is "The terrorists are bad guys who hate freedom and we're the good guys who love freedom and we're gonna get 'em."

A lot of people in the human potential movement and a number of social activists have written about the attack. I like what most of these folks are saying. I find it easy to fantasize about these wise people being in charge.

Plato's ideal of government by philosopher kings comes to mind. These are our philosopher kings and queens. I can't keep from imagining a new government for the United States and the United Nations in which people like Deepak Chopra, Neale Donald Walsch, Gay and Kathryn Hendricks, Marianne Williamson, Denise Breton, Christopher Largent, David Korten, David Edwards, the Dalai Lama, and others like them, actually occupy positions of influence and power. I mean in actual government. In actual positions of power in the way the world is run. Like, Marianne Williamson as Secretary of Defense; Deepak Chopra as Surgeon General; Denise Breton as Attorney General; David Korten as Secretary of Commerce; Gay Hendricks as Secretary of Health and Human Services; Tom Robbins as Secretary of Home Security, and on and on.

A lot of people in our radical honesty community have been e-mailing us at headquarters, or calling, or forwarding e-mails from other writers and public figures. We have been watching TV a lot. In the first week or so after the tragedy hundreds of friends e-mailed us (and we them) about what has occurred, what preceded it and what actions might actually bring about an end to all the killing.

We have been synthesizing the input from friends around the country, and I am grateful to be able to include a lot of what that conversation has been about, for the final content of this book. I have been constantly amazed at and moved by the brilliance and compassion of our community of friends.

What I think is this: After all the hurting and all the anger, the opportunity of the tragedy is for us to *bring to bear the wisdom of compassion to the struggle between the haves and the have nots concerning materialism and its defense.*

In the deeper discussion it is clear that there is an important broad agreement: Of course we condemn terrorism. But we also see that we have to get beyond simple moral condemnation of terrorism, in order to look at what it is and where it comes from. We are sorry for the people and their loved ones who have been caused death and suffering by the terrorists. We are grateful for and touched by the kindness and generosity of the thousands upon thousands of people who have volunteered to help in any way they can. We are also full of admiration and gratitude for the sacrifices of the people who were killed while attempting to rescue others or help them escape.

We wish the whole thing had not happened and would like to do what we can to prevent it from happening again. We have to start by understanding as much as we can about where all of this comes from. And we agree that we must start on that task by listening to what the terrorists have to say and trying to understand what they hate us for and why they want to make war on us.

Now, I must speak for myself in the first person, not as a representative of a synthesis of a larger community, although many of this community of conversation on the Internet do agree with me. I, too, am sorry for what happened to all those people who were killed in those planes and buildings and for the pain of all who loved them that continues and will continue for such a long time.

I am also sorry for the death, destruction and oppression caused by the United States of America and its allies, prior to, during and after the terrorist attack on New York and Washington. I am also sorry for the intensification of that suffering which our country is currently engaged in, and constantly gearing up to continue. I would also like to do what I can to prevent that. The suffering caused by the U.S. and its allies has been, and will probably continue to be, much greater and more persistent than that caused by the terrorists. This will continue to be true unless or until some terrorist among the enemies of the U.S. escalates back, and brings a hydrogen bomb or deadly virus in a suitcase to one of our major cities.

I would be opposed to this kind of warfare between terrorists and anti-terrorists, whether or not they were using my money to do it with, and since they are, I resent them for that as well. I am a materialist. So are all the participants in the military industrial conspiracy in the United States and England. So are the poor and starving people of the world, most of all, because they can't afford not to be. This is what creates the context in which terrorism thrives. That includes the State terrorism of the United States of America.

We have to look at things the way they are. To start with, terrorism is an option of war. Like many of war's grisly options, it is unspeakably insane and horrible, but it is there, nevertheless, along with the rest of the list of humanity's cruelest stupidities. When folks are poor and oppressed and they wish to attack people who are rich and well defended, the only thing they have as weapons are their bodies and their commitment. If they are willing to sacrifice their lives they can fight their enemy, using the enemy's equipment, and take lives from their enemy. Terrorism is their best option, given the decision to make war on their oppressors.

The terrorists attacked the twin towers of the World Trade Center and the Pentagon to make a statement about what they hate and what they see as wrong with the way the world is run these days. I agree with them, fundamentally, in their analysis. I agree with their judgment of the evil perpetrated by the world-wide economic order, controlled by the wealthy, maintained in secrecy and defended by military might. I also believe that if Colin Powell were in the terrorists' shoes he would do the same as they have. In fact, he is in their shoes and he is going about doing the same thing they have done, right now.

I prefer the option of solutions other than war, whether it be war in the form of terrorism or war in the form of the military-industrial complex. The multi-national corporate bottom line is not a sufficient primary value to provide satisfaction for more than about one per cent of the population of the world. In fact, in it's current form, it requires that the poor continue getting poorer and multiply and the rich continue getting richer and decrease.

Terrorists will not go away, whether the U.S. and its allies and those who have chosen or been forced to align with them make war on terrorism or not. The military industrial war machine will not "conquer terrorism." Quite the contrary, it will continue the context, the milieu in which terrorism resides and therefore, without a doubt, contribute to the continuation and expansion of terrorism.

The context in which terrorism resides is the same context in which the military industrial complex resides. The secret meetings and plans of terrorists are held in the same framework as the secret meetings of the 36 separate secret agencies of the United States of America, the joint chiefs of staff, the Cabinet, the closed meetings of Congress, the behind the scenes conversations between lobbyists and legislators, etc.

If we really want to do something about terrorism we have to start listening to terrorists as well as to ourselves. We have to lead with our hearts and follow with our minds. We have to come to an understanding of our common humanity and our common limitations of perspective. We have to tell the truth about what we think and feel and plan to do. *We have to give up secrecy.* We have to create a new context within which we all live, based on really knowing what we all want, as well as what we all have to offer each other.

Here is the wisdom whose time has come. Or I should say, this is an idea whose time may get here if we don't all kill each other first. It's this: We, who are human beings, are all alike. We are all, in common, holy human prototypes of aliveness. We are the ones on the earth who notice and think. We see and hear and touch and taste and feel things and we dream things up about what to do. Since way before there were billions of us who had to figure out how to get along together, we have been making up rules and traditions and conventions about how to get along together. We just made it up. The way we do things together is just something we made up together. Most of these ways were made up by people who are already dead now. *It is not working. We need to make something else up.*

When we make up something new, we might consider this, particularly in the light of how our government is responding to the terrorist attack. The terrorists attacked symbols. Killing people was secondary, just to underline the importance of the attack on "the evil of Western wealth and corruption." They wanted to kill the World Trade Center and the Pentagon. Just as Colin Powell and Bush the elder killed 60,000 teenagers and way more than 6,000 civilians and children in the "Gulf War" and left Saddam Hussein to live on, to kill more.

We have killed hundreds of thousands more, mostly children, by starving them to death and depriving them of medical supplies since the Gulf War, with an economic boycott that punishes the poor. We did this not to just kill those people, but to show that the "evil invader" could not get by with his "evil invasion." In fact it was better that he lived, so we could be sure we had taught him a lesson. And we still can keep teaching a lesson to the populace that "allows him to remain in power."

It was the principle of the thing. Like the President said the other night: "This Evil will not go unpunished!" The principle of the thing and the war on Evil was more important than the lives of the people involved on either side. First you say how terrible it was, then you say how the terrorists are evil, then you perpetrate more terror.

In all of these cases, it is the symbols being more important that the lives of people. When our leaders, via the CIA, trained Saddam Hussein and many of his colleagues, *in secret,* to oppose Iran, and trained most of Bin Laden's current cohorts, *in secret,* to defeat the Russians in Afghanistan, it was also for symbolic reasons. It seemed like a good idea at the time to "defeat Communism" or "extremism" or some other "ism."

None of these choices were ever subject to democratic review. Not that they might not have been approved anyway, given the gullible numb nuts that make up the majority of the populace. It just pisses me off that the hypocritical so-called leaders in Congress and the Executive office insist on calling this a democracy when *we never even get a chance to talk about what is actually going on when it is going on.* These choices just never were discussed openly or voted on. They were done in secret, in our name, using our money, without our review or approval, to protect and defend us against symbolic enemies. We were told about some of it later. Much later. After it was too late. And some of it we still don't know about. Secret violence, secret war and study of war, secret support in the form of weapons for war, done in our name (without being subject to review, public debate, vote, conversation, or review in the media), done on our behalf, for our own good (in the judgment of our caretakers in secret meetings) all have been the source of a lot of shit we have had to put up with later—like, for example, the bombing of the World Trade Center and the Pentagon.

So the dance goes on. Most of us are more than eager to join in the grieving sentimental hate-filled orgasm of righteousness against the perpetrators of evil who have murdered the innocent, and smite them back tenfold. Millions of us support with our hearts full of feeling, the same bunch of fat men creating new and ever more bloody scenes of sadistic vengeance. I, personally, hate those hate-filled ignorant jerks. The ones on our side as well as the ones on the so-called "other" side. But I am *not* willing to actually kill them for what they represent. It's tempting, but I'm not going to do it. I'll cuss them and holler at them and name call them and damn them to hell and maybe slap the shit out of one or two of them if I get a chance, but I'm not going to kill them. I might even get over some of my righteousness and forgive them and have an honest conversation with them. That is a minor but important difference between the terrorists, including our own terrorists, and me. And I know I'm not alone. I think it is a minor but important difference between millions of us and our leaders. There are millions who are not even as mean as me. But there are many more millions who are angry, righteous and not informed in the least about the actual conditions that have created and continue to create terrorism. They're usually the ones who wave their flags the hardest and brag about their "patriotism."

As of the first week of October 2001, according to the Gallup poll, George W. Bush had a ninety percent approval rating, the highest ever recorded for a president. Eighty-two percent of the populace was in favor of making war on Afghanistan. The warriors are dancing around the fire preparing to attack, and then attacking. The whole tribe seems to be in agreement with them. I am not.

The U.S. immediately made Pakistan stop sending aid to hungry people in Afghanistan. About seven days later, the number of innocent people killed since the morning of September 11 had doubled, from 5,000 to 10,000. That increase in number, our share of the total, was mostly children who starved to death. Innocent people are being killed by the hundreds on a daily basis since we have begun "the war on terrorism." The military mind and the militant mind are simply not, as we say in Texas, all ate up with compassion.

I realize George W. Bush is doing the best he can, as are his helpers. And I do feel sorry for him and understand his anger and his hurt and his way of thinking about it and the limitations of the choices he seems to have at hand. I do consider it extremely unfortunate that such arrogance wields such power. I think it is up to us to create other options in the media and the minds of other people in order to alter the path of escalation our leaders are on, which will lead more quickly than anyone suspects, to tragedies that will make the recent tragedy seem small in comparison.

In a typical revolution you kill the leaders, take control, and become leaders like them. In the revolution of consciousness it is not that easy or satisfying. In the revolution of consciousness we have to use that energy to *talk about what is so* and *make up something new.* We have to make up a new model for how we live together. And the sooner we do so the sooner the madness of escalating terrorism, state terrorism included, will come to an end.

We are doing just that—talking about what is so and making up a new model. The new model makers are at work and they are you and me. In the dialogue that follows in this book, Neale and I wish to further the work of making up a new model for how to live together, based on spiritual awareness and compassion. Please take your time and read this. Send letters in response to this to us to our websites. Keep up the good work. Keep this conversation going. It is the only way we have of making up a new way to live together.

The woods we have to go into are deep. These folks, whose quotations follow, mark the beginning of the path—the start of making up something new.

> "If we continue to think in terms of a Cartesian dualism of mind vs. matter, we shall probably also come to see the world in terms of God versus man, élite versus people, chosen race versus others; nation versus nation; and man versus environment. It is doubtful whether a species *having both an advanced technology* and *this strange way of looking at the world* can endure." (Italics mine)
>
> Gregory Bateson, "Steps to an Ecology of Mind"

> "The ultimate weakness of violence is that it is a descending spiral, begetting the very thing it seeks to destroy. Instead of diminishing evil, it multiplies it . . . Through violence you may murder the hater, but you do not murder hate. In fact, violence merely increases hate . . . Returning violence for violence multiplies violence, adding deeper darkness to a night already devoid of stars. Darkness cannot drive out hate; only love can do that."
>
> Rev. Dr. Martin Luther King, Jr.

"If we take an eye for an eye, soon the whole world will be blind."

Gandhi

The following quotation is from my friend, Doris Haddock, otherwise known as Granny D. She is one of my living heroes. This ninety-two year-old-woman walked all the way across America to draw attention to the need for campaign finance reform. I walked the last five miles with her and got arrested in her name in the Rotunda of the Capitol that day. The trial transcript and commentary of Chapter Ten came from that arrest.

When I got out of jail seven hours later she kissed me right on the lips and thanked me for what I had done. SHE thanked ME, for Christ's sake. I cried like a baby and didn't wash my face for a week where she kissed me. She was there again at the protest rally against the Bush inauguration and she spoke so eloquently I cried my heart out again. I love her. When I grow up I want to be just like her.

"While the surgeons will cut, others will look to a deeper question: How can such cold-bloodedness arise in the hearts of our fellow men? As the nutritionist examines the lifestyle that may lead to disease, we begin to ask: What can we do in the future so that love and respect are nurtured in the place of hatred? Surely we cannot kill our way to love and respect, where our only true security resides.

"The surgeons will undoubtedly have their way for a time. Those who seek true security must not stand aside in silence. Those who know that international justice is the only road to international peace must continue to speak their minds. It is not un-American to do so. It is, on the contrary, un-American to fall into a state of fascism, where our civil liberties are forsaken and the human needs of Americans and of people around the globe are forgotten.

"The secretaries and file clerks and young executives in the stricken office buildings, and the children and mothers and fathers and sisters and brothers aboard those four airplanes would not have been the targets of hatred, had we Americans better expressed our highest values throughout the world—had our government expressed in all its actions the fairness and generosity that characterize our people. That disconnection between our people and our government does not excuse the cold mass-murders committed by terrorists, but it helps explain it, and we cannot stop it if we do not understand it.

"Let us pray that some of our leaders are wiser than that, and can see that the real road to security does not lead us to places like Kabul with our mops and brooms, but to places like Langley, and to the mammoth political fundraising events where our representatives are bought away from us.

"In my long walk across the U.S., and in my everyday experiences, I know that Americans are kindhearted and do not wish to colonize and exploit any other people on earth. Our central question—the question that will determine the security of our cities in the future—is this: Can those American values be expressed by the American government? Can we be more a government of our people? Can we get the greedy, short-sighted interests out from between us and our elected representatives?

"Our struggle for campaign finance reform and other democratic reforms will now take a back seat as blood and its disciples have their day. But until we clean up our government, we will all be the targets of rising international rage, and our children and grandchildren are not safe."

Doris "Granny D" Haddock

18

A Conversation About

A World in Crisis

NDW: The very first question in this book (Neale was holding up his very newest release: "Conversations with God for Teens") is completely and utterly applicable to what's going on with the Taliban right now. The first question asked in the book is: "Why is the world the way it is? Why can't we stop the killing and the suffering? Why can't we find a way to get along with each other—to love each other? Is it always going to have to be this way? Is there nothing anyone can do to change it? Am I just going to have to give up hope for trying to make things different because it's not going to work anyway? Okay, God, if there is a god, what's up?" It's right on target. It's just amazing. Part of the answer that came to me was:

"Your species has not been able to stop the killing and the suffering because your species has a killing and suffering mentality. Those who have come before you have believed that killing is justified as a means of resolving their disagreements or getting what they want or think they need. They have also believed that suffering was a normal part of life. Some of them even have said that it is required by God.

"It is from these beliefs that the present human experience has arisen. It is out of these understandings that your elders create their every day reality, and yours. You can find a way to get along, to be nice to each other and to love each other but it would require you to give up these beliefs and a great many others and it's not something that those who have come before you have been willing to do."

I read it last night and thought, "Good heavens, that's right on the money."

BB: That whole sort of "set theory" that has to do with the Judeo-Christian tradition is the hardest thing to overcome, I think, because . . .

NDW: The what theory?

BB: The set theory. The way that you operate according to a limited set or perspective. A mind frame. You look for suffering, and once you believe it's something that's required, you end up finding what you look for.

NDW: Not only that, but if you don't find it, you'll create it. If you can't create it you'll make it up and pretend that it's there. If you can't create it in reality, you'll do anything not to disavow or invalidate your prior thought about it. First you'll see it wherever you can find it; if you can't find it you'll create it and if you can't create it, you'll make it up and pretend it's there.

BB: Right.

NDW: So it's there, whether it's there or not! I had a mother-in-law who did that wonderfully. She went through all those three steps, and if there wasn't any suffering she'd go into an act, her story, and pretend she was suffering. Everyone would say, "Oh, Ma!" If there isn't anything current you can always go back to remembered suffering and make it very real, because the mind doesn't know the difference.

BB: You know, when someone has their appendix out it's called an appendectomy. When they have their tonsils out it's called a tonsillectomy. What do you call it when you have a growth removed from your head?

NDW: I'm afraid to ask . . .

BB: A haircut! (Laughter) You see, it was the set. We can have a set provided for us in just a few seconds. That set I provided for you there had you thinking "medical terminology." If I'd just said, "What do you call it when you have a growth cut off your head?" you might think it was a little weird, but you'd probably have said "haircut" as one of your first options, but once I provided a set, it would become an option only far down the road. You'd have to drop the box that we set up together in conversation about what to expect. So, what we do, apparently, is to live constantly in previously existing sets. We have bigger sets and little subsets.

NDW: Well, we have to, to some degree. These are the contextual frameworks in which we hold the experience of life. And naturally, it's necessary to create some of those in order for us to experience life in the relative world. But the danger is in *not knowing that we're making it all up.* The danger is, as I point out in "Communion with God," not understanding that it's all an illusion. What we have an opportunity to do, is to work *with* the illusion but not be *within* it. Right now, we're like a magician who's forgotten his own tricks.

BB: Ain't it the truth! I've had conversations with a number of people since September 11th and for many of us there's a slight discomfort that seems to be there about what we see and hear in the media and in the world. People tell me that they see all the flag-waving and when they go down the street and see an American flag and they see the signs that say, "God Bless America," and they see the quotes from the National Anthem and the replays on television, they feel a little bit uneasy. It is a little reminiscent of films of the Third Reich. It reminds us of the days of Joe McCarthy, or the prison camps for Japanese-American citizens in California during World War II.

There are many other instances when people rallied around a lesser group of human beings, separated themselves out as special in response to another group doing the same, and adopted the mind set that we are good and they are evil. Why not say, "God Bless the World" instead of "God Bless America"? Why not have a flag that has a picture of the globe, of the whole world on it, rather than have a flag of the United States of America? Why not have a way of acknowledging, first, our common humanity and, second, our subset as Americans?

The question is, which is the subset? Are we first Americans, and the subset is our common humanity? Or are we first human beings, and the subset is Americans?

I'm interested in how people get to where they can change sets or change the arrangement of what subsumes what. I want to have a conversation in the large world out there about perspectives and how to change perspectives and not be limited to a given perspective. As we know, limited and closed perspectives are damned dangerous.

NDW: You're talking about what the movie industry simply calls POV—Point of View. And, this is what we did in Korea a few months ago when the New Millennium Peace Foundation, created by Grand Master Seun Heung Lee and me, sponsored the Humanity Conference. Some 12,000 people came to the closing ceremony in a stadium in Seoul and recited a Declaration of Humanity.

The Declaration said exactly what you just said here, in a few sentences. It was a little more poetic because we had time to create it, but it had that declaration of independence ring to it. It simply said that we declare that we are first and foremost universal humans, members of the—what you would call the primary set, not the subset. That we are Earth Humans.

What Grand Master Lee and I hope to do is create a worldwide movement to generate a new thought about ourselves, and therefore a new category into which we can pour our combined collective experience, that we would call Earth Humans. We're asking people to declare themselves Earth Humans. And not to give up our Americanism or our Koreanism or any other "ism" that we want to experience, but to place them in their proper context. All things in their proper context, so that when we face some kind of collectively experienced threat, or danger that we respond to it from that point of view.

BB: Good for you. More power to you.

NDW: I must say that geopolitically on the planet, in the aftermath of the September 11th incident, many governments of the world have done just that. NATO, to their credit said that an attack on one is an attack on all. And other major governments, as well as thirty nations (around the world in the area of the Middle East) have also indicated that this particular behavior on the part of the terrorists, regardless of their grievances, is not an appropriate way to resolve those grievances. Even those who in some small ways might agree with points of view held by those people who are terrorizing the world have also openly condemned terrorism. Syria, surprisingly, is an example, even though there are some terrorist bases in Syria. Apparently they are willing to train them but not have them carry anything out. Small level of what appears on the surface to be hypocrisy unless we look deeper into what's happening in Syria.

The point that I'm making is that geopolitically, through this coalition of nation states that the U.S. and Great Britain have managed to stitch together, there seems to be the beginning of that kind of generalized response, "Wait a minute, this is a crime against humanity."

It's natural, however, whether it's in the United States or anywhere else to begin waving a flag. All animals rush to their nest when there's any kind of danger. It's just instinctual. So we go back to the nest and hide behind Mama and in this case Mama just happens to look a whole lot like Uncle Sam and a flag that's red white and blue. So this is not, I don't think, an effective time to convince people to change their POV, to have a new point of view about it.

It should be our second-level response, after our first-level reaction of this government and the world has been expressed. I've been saying in my talks all over the country, that if we must have a second-level reaction following the natural and instinctual reaction, it couldn't be denied if you wanted it to be. It's natural and instinctual, the truth of which is that you're going to defend yourself vociferously if not viciously.

BB: Well, the September 11 tragedy didn't just happen out of nowhere.

It was not a first time event, just a bigger event and closer to home. It resided in a chain of unjust slaughter and surreptitious murder, punishment through starvation and more subtle economic violence in which the United States has been complicit and a full participant. This terrorist act as well as our response to it are ongoing vicious responses to previous actions. These immediate reactions, whether natural or not, are what continue the ongoing stream of violence.

So, I say, whether it is a natural reaction or not, a first level response creating more first level responses has to be intervened with somehow to stop the chain. The so-called "war on terrorism" creates more terrorists in larger numbers than those that are eliminated, and continues the cycle of violence and counter violence.

NDW: Having already done that now though, I think if we don't go to the second level, which is exactly what you're talking about, and rearrange our idea about who we are, what we're doing and life itself, we're going to continue to be in attack and self-defense mode until the end of time, or until the next attack becomes an attack of such magnitude that the end of time will have arrived.

BB: Exactly.

NDW: I think that the challenge before the human species is to find within it a certain leadership. And it's clearly not going to come from the political establishment. It's not going to come from the economic establishment. It's not going to come from the establishment of educators and absolutely not going to come from organized religion.

Organized religion will not send its leadership out to the public to say; "We were wrong about a lot of stuff, folks. In fact, it isn't the way we thought it was." Even if the religious leaders felt that in some instances this was true, that they'd been wrong about some things, they couldn't possibly say that to their congregates and their followers, for fear that they would lose their constituency. Where are the internationally known Muslim spiritual leaders standing up shoulder to shoulder with Christian leaders and Jewish leaders and leaders of all faith traditions at a major press conference in some more or less neutral city?

They should be issuing a joint statement to the world: "We say and we declare to our followers that however else you want to interpret the scriptures of our various faiths, killing each other to resolve our grievances is inappropriate. So this is not a time for Muslims everywhere to declare *jihad,* nor for people of any faith tradition to do so."

I'm waiting for that statement to be made jointly by the world's religious leaders standing side by side, but that event will probably not happen.

BB: I agree that what's critical is phase two, after the initial reaction. Phase one has already happened and is still happening. But the question is how long will it take to enter into phase two? Actually, I think we're entering into phase two right now. How much of phase one and how much of phase two will happen this next year following the terrorist attack in New York and Washington—and in the years following? This is truly a critical time. And I also agree that that leadership must be found or created. We very much need a leader who doesn't come from the usual fields of choice.

NDW: This is what Jean Houston calls "The Open Moment."

BB: Yes, this is the open moment.

NDW: She says that the open moment occurs when our need is so great that we can't help but open our eyes, even when we don't want to.

BB: Yeah, this is one of them. And we're speaking right now, hopefully, into that open listening. It's not completely open yet, but it's there. And there is a set for what defines power that has to be transcended. When you talk about our standard categories, there are religious leaders and there are political leaders, economic leaders and so forth.

We are not going to get the institutional religious leaders to come out with a strong stance because they will be concerned about their constituency. You're probably not going to get the business leaders to take a strong stance because they're concerned about their profit, and have a vested interest in the economic order remaining the same, and so forth. So the question arises, "Where does actual power to bring about social change come from?"

It doesn't appear to be political power because people get elected and nothing much happens. It doesn't even appear to be economic power. Economic power is the ongoing show of the degree of difficulty for people to stay alive and have a quality of life that is not painful in various ways in different geographic locations.

We have a chance to look now at a perspective that is truly a world-wide perspective. As I mentioned before, the largest economic enterprise on planet earth is illegal drugs, most of them painkillers. One of the largest legal enterprises is called the pharmaceutical industry, with the great majority of products being painkillers and anti-depressants. So we can wonder, if there's some way, with the tragedy in New York and Washington and Pennsylvania, since we have now been made to suffer, that we have an opportunity to identify with all human suffering? Because we have become aware of suffering in a new way. This very suffering could direct our attention so that our effort against terrorism is an effort to deal with the context within which terrorism resides; the battle between the have's and the have not's. It's the battle between the people with one set of survival skills and perspectives versus the people with another set.

The degree of hatred that people have for America has something to do with what we are able to get by with in their view. We get by without suffering along with them in the same way, when they have to suffer. And we constantly show off how we get to play (although frequently it is only a new form of suffering) without worrying about survival of our loved ones and ourselves. Going back to Maslow's hierarchy of needs: When you are concerned with biological survival your perspective is limited to obtaining food and shelter and making a lot of babies so that one may survive to care for you if you are lucky enough to live to be old. Once you have enough to eat and a place to stay, you then become concerned with social acceptance. Finally, when you are comfortable about social acceptance you can then worry about meaning.

People are coming from quite different sets in these differing circumstances. So, for example, people who grow opium poppies to make a living are not much concerned with the sufferings of inner city families and the breakdown of the social order in the United States.

One of the things that could get a lot of us on the same page would be for the U.S. to go ahead and feed the world, and help put in place structures that help the world to continue to feed itself. There are plenty of resources to do so. It would only take a minuscule amount of the immense defense budget. That won't handle all suffering, of course. But it gets at the baseline of the most critical, terrifying and fatal kind.

I've been a therapist for over thirty years and I know lots of Americans. I know plenty of people who have plenty of money who suffer like hell all the time. The degree of suffering is not a one to one ratio regarding whether you have money or not. It's whether you have the ability to escape the sets of your mind or not. Individual neurosis is the same as the social milieu. People have standards that they're holding themselves to and which they won't let up on, and standards that they hold other people to that they won't let up about. So, they're miserable because they can't get the world of reality to match their standards for what they think that reality should be, and they make miserable those who don't meet their expectations.

So, the question is, can we have, in this open moment, a unique opportunity to talk about suffering in a kind of Buddhist way? What we could do, as the richest and most powerful nation in the world, is say to all of humanity, including ourselves: "What can we do to have less suffering, to transcend suffering and have our current suffering lead to a contribution to less suffering?" There are lots of ways we can actually bring about less suffering.

NDW: That is, I think, a profound question. I think you've articulated what the moment is begging to know. I was waiting to see if you had an answer to propose, when you asked the question, "Where will the leadership come from? You said it won't come from the religious or economic or political or the education establishment. I thought you were going to propose where it might come from, or where the power does lie.

BB: I think it's going to come from people who are aware of the fundamental issue of compassion and suffering regardless of what particular sub-enterprise they happen to be part of. There needs to be a new coalition here, some from business, some from religion, some from spiritual leaders that are not affiliated with any institutions, some from religious institutions who see beyond the doctrine, some people in government . . . but what has to be the unifying principle is a concern about suffering that comes from compassion. Remember Margaret Meade saying, "Never doubt that a small group of committed individuals can change the world; it's the only thing that ever does." Are there enough of us, regardless from what walk of life who, through what we've experienced from this terrorist attack can allow ourselves to feel, after the initial reaction, and identity with all suffering? Does it give us a sense of the ongoing nature of the insecurity of most of the people in the world? Are we willing to do the tasks of taking responsibility for what we know is asked of us? Particularly, those of us here in America. We can't feel secure in the way we could before, and won't be able to, ever again. Now we know we're vulnerable to a terrorist attack.

I think that the first reaction is creating more terrorists as we speak. I think that making a war on terrorism with military might creates more terrorists, so we will always have a dependable supply of terrorists to continue coming forward. There's got to be a new affiliation of people capable of a new perspective that cuts across "isms" and borders. And it will have to come from citizens of the world for whom affiliation with lesser identities, like political, economic, literary, religious or even spiritual roles is less important than their identity as human beings. Let me talk about an example.

I was talking to Gay Hendricks and to Bill Galt in southern California, and to a number of other people about using the 2004 presidential campaign as a future organizing point. We want to start putting together a cabinet that we would consider to be ideal leaders. Some would come from business, some would come from writers and seminar leaders like us, some would be politicians, some would come from comedians—I particularly like comedians.

NDW: (Laughter) Oh, I thought those were the same . . . they're called politicians. (Laughter) Okay, go ahead.

BB: And some would be artists and performers. But they would all be folks with a transcendent perspective.

NDW: I've decided that I want to be elevated to the vice-presidential candidate. I've changed my mind. I was going for Secretary of State.

BB: You want to be the Vice-Presidential candidate for this new cabinet?

NDW: Yes, that way I'd get elevated to President if anything happens and I'd get to be in the position of making some major changes . . . go ahead.

BB: Okay, so what I'm saying is that we put together a cabinet and then we look for a leader. We're talking about asking Oprah and talking about seeing what we think of Jesse Ventura, since he's probably going to run anyway. Through this cabinet of volunteers for particular posts, we would have this combined contribution of a lot of fairly powerful people. Powerful with regard to the ability to shift, invent sets, live outside the box and come up with a new unique, creative solution, based on compassion and a desire to contribute to the lessening of suffering.

NDW: Ralph Nader falls very close to that.

BB: You bet! And I'd love to have Ralph Nader come in on the conversation, and John Hagelin, too. I don't think either one of them are good enough political candidates for President, but I would love for them to be in on the dialogue and become part of this kitchen cabinet. If we had people who formerly have made some impact on a lot of people, and who have been heard in some degree espousing a larger perspective, as members of this cabinet, we could all campaign for the new perspective. I, by the way, only want to be ambassador to the UN and head of the CIA. That's all I want. (Laughter)

NDW: Not much to ask.

BB: No, not much to ask. I want to be head of the CIA because I love revealing secrets. (Laughter) I just can't wait to get in there and say, "Hey, look at this, this has been classified for twenty years. Look at what we did!" I'd come out with a new one every day.

NDW: You see, transparency—utter transparency in the conduct of human affairs—would change the conduct of human affairs.

BB: Wouldn't it! Absolutely. That very principle, if we were to say, "Let's all talk about this!"—as members of the Cabinet; we don't have a President or Vice-President yet, we might have you as the vice-presidential candidate—but we'd hold this conversation about having a primary value that looks at everything in the light of say, compassion, for example. If you use compassion as the primary value and you look at everything in the light of that, you find out that mostly, secrecy leads to a lot of really bad trouble. It was the secrecy of the CIA with regard to hundreds of individual acts that definitely helped bring about terrorism in the world.

NDW: Yes, of course, that results in anger and bitterness and produces terrorism. Terrorism emerges from anger, and irrationally so, perhaps, or perhaps not. People have an experience then they're afraid that it's going to happen again, then they become angry because it does, and become terrorists because they can't stop it. It's quite simple. Then when you go back to first cause, you see, "Oh, I get it," the first cause was quite preventable, even though now it looks as if you can't stop the cycle.

BB: But there's a perspective on the cycle. If we were engaged in conversation about a perspective on the cycle that is just and acknowledges what has occurred. As long as the conversation stays with a big perspective on the whole cycle of what happens, it doesn't make any difference who's right and who's wrong—or how many different approaches we take. The thing to be solved is not just the immediate reaction to who got hurt right now. It is, rather, how to do something about the whole cycle.

NDW: What should be the prime value, though? What was the term that you used? The first value? The context in which to hold everything? The prime value?

BB: I like compassion.

NDW: Compassion is your thought about it?

BB: Just because of the eloquence of most of the Buddhists who talk about it. For example, Thich Nhat Hanh. Did you see his poem about the September 11th events?

NDW: Yes. He's written a marvelous book by the way, called, simply, "Anger," and it's very relevant to this moment. It just came out about five months ago . . . from the time of this recording now in October. It's quite extraordinary. Thich Nhat Hanh is a wonderful writer. He's very simple, very direct, and very straightforward.

BB: He is.

NDW: He talks about anger and says a lot of the things you say a lot, Brad. It sounded like a softer, kinder, gentler, version of Brad Blanton. It truly did. I felt well, he's read Brad's books and just put some mayonnaise on it, made it a little sweeter. (Laughter)

BB: Mine already has enough mayonnaise on it.

NDW: No, yours has horseradish. (Laughter)

BB: Okay.

NDW: It's a book I recommend to everyone. I've been proposing a prime value, or a first thought that informs every other thought, or a first or primary set. I think that what we're missing here is unity. The prime value must be the prime reality, that there is only one of us and we think that we are separate from each other. I think that one of the reasons that we don't, ordinarily at least, except under the most extraordinary of circumstances, harm members of our own family is because it is clear that at some level we share a common experience.

One might say loosely that we share a oneness with members of our family and with our dearest and deepest loved ones. That's certainly the reason why we don't harm ourselves, except under the most extraordinary circumstances. We don't normally take a hatchet and cut off our left hand with our right. Under most circumstances we wouldn't do that because in that instance we're very clear that it's one being, the left hand and the right hand belong to the same body.

BB: It may be only a matter of words here, but the experience of being one with another, and with all of being, is probably the best working definition of compassion we could come up with. One might say, if not through compassion, how else can one have an experience of oneness through which it can become the primary set? For me it is a real experience to recognize the being over there as being just like me.

NDW: Largely, human beings don't deliberately damage themselves. Though they'll much more freely damage others. If we could simply enlarge the definition of self, if we could expand people's concept or definition of what self-interest is, then that I think is where most of the social scientists are going.

BB: I agree.

NDW: Thinkers like Michael Lerner, Jean Houston, Barbara Marx Hubbard, Peter Russell and social constructionists of that sort, are talking about simply expanding the definition of self-interest and changing the bottom line in terms of *what we mean by what profits all of us,* and who all of us are. I think that that is a larger contextual field than some subset beneath it like fairness. Fairness has nothing to do with it. I don't not hit my left hand with a hammer in my right because I want to be fair to my left hand.

BB: I don't think so either.

NDW: Or even because I want to be compassionate. It gets down to avoiding pain. It gets down to the most basic element. It's the pain/pleasure principle.

So as soon as I see in my mind that that Being sitting over there is me, and if I hit him hard enough with a hammer, ultimately he's going to hit me back.

We talked about this in the first part of the book. Therefore in the truest sense, I'm hitting myself. That's what creates the cycle. As soon as we get to "Oh, I get it, when I hit him, I'm hitting me. It just takes a while for it to get back over here." But it's absolutely what's going on; we're absolutely seeing that right now.

BB: Or even to say, "He is just like me and when I hit him the hurt I cause hurts him and me both, whether I get the reaction of him hurting me back or not." It's even more immediate; you don't even have to wait for the reaction. You can identify with the pain at the moment you cause it in another. We get to recognize that causing another human being pain—causing ourselves pain—that is compassion. It's not whether or not we get that they'll hit us back, but the identification with their pain that generates the possibility of Oneness as a primary experience.

NDW: So, if we need to change that idea of our disunity (what "Communion With God" calls the illusion of disunity, the idea that we are separate from each other) because the illusion is very, very strong. Once when we step outside of that illusion, we suddenly begin behaving entirely differently toward people, and that's demonstrable. When we have those feelings that we call "falling in love," we behave demonstrably different toward the person who is the object of our affection. The question becomes, why can't everyone be the object of our affection?

BB; Well, I think that's a great question. I think that defining into a smaller subset the "us" and "them" is what makes sure that we're not identified with the people in the other group—in order to preserve our own separateness. We preserve our separateness to preserve our identity, and we identify ourselves by being different than that other group.

So if we say that fundamentally we're the same, that we're all part of one being, and that we operate out of being, and that we're common manifestations of that being, then what does it change about the political and economic order? Well, what it changes is, a kind of honoring of being, which is what the Buddhist definition of compassion is, basically, the honoring of Being.

There are lots of different words for this, but what I think could be the primary focus of a group of compassionate-thought leaders, who became a cabinet looking for a candidate, would be that we're looking for opportunities to honor being. If someone was holding the ground on that perspective, holding the ground with regard to unity and compassion, then everything discussed in terms of future actions would be subject to review in the light of that perspective.

No matter what the process or topic of discussion, if we brought an issue before the Cabinet, then that criterion of unity or compassion would always be there. And we ask, "What does that look like, the profits we're taking, the arms that we're producing and so forth, in terms of our goal of compassionate awareness of unity?"

You know, there is this argument that it's not guns that kill people; it's people who kill people. But if we have a whole stack of guns here and we get mad at each other, are we more likely to kill each other? The answer is, yes, we are. We've been endlessly supplying weaponry to really poor people so they can fight with each other in endless power struggles. We, as a nation, generate lots of arms and lots of things that people can kill each other with in the world. A lot of our resources come from, and depend on the fact that we produce lots and lots and lots of those things.

The Cold War has been over for ten years. We still have the same military budget we had when the Cold War was going on. We need to look at this assignment and allocation of resources (politically and economically) in light of these questions: "Is this a manifestation of unity or disunity? Is it contributing to the illusion of disunity, or to the accomplishment of acknowledged common unity?" A lot of our power, especially our financial power, has gone to generate disunity, rather than to acknowledge our common unity.

NDW: There's no question about that, Brad. A recent study conducted by social scientists concluded that we, the world community, could embark on a six-year plan that would eradicate virtually every major problem that civilization is now facing. Within six years, with concerted research and the application of knowledge that emerges from that research, we could effectively eliminate the major problems we now see on our planet, including the problems that most of society acknowledges, such as hunger and poverty, and also the problems that seem to threaten us from the fringe of our awareness. There's the ozone layer problem; the problem of deforestation of the planet; the topsoil problem; the issue of how we're using our resources; and all the other environmental problems. This study indicated that in six years' time we could eliminate all these problems, and we could do that *with a sum of money equal to just one annual allocation the world now devotes to weapons of war.*

So all we would have to do is say, look, for one year we'll take a hiatus and we won't spend any money. We'll keep everything in place but we won't spend any money. We'll just take that one-year's expenditure and apply it to solving the problems that require us to defend ourselves against war, and against the attacks from each other that arise from these very problems. The source of these problems would be eliminated, or at least vastly reduced. And the compelling question, and you've just asked it, is: When will humanity decide that maybe we're approaching the challenge of peacefully coexisting together? When will we decide that there must be another way to do this and a different way to focus our resources?

I think that is something that must emerge from new leadership.

We have to have new leadership. I love your idea of having a new cabinet and president here in this country, and I'm willing to sign onto that. Not that I think it has any realistic chance, but it gives us an opportunity to make a huge statement. New leadership has to emerge from somewhere and if nobody else is going to do it, we are. Just to place the question before the minds of the American people.

Across the world on my tours I've been arguing that what we need is new spiritual leadership, and that it's not going to come from the places where leadership traditionally comes from. I say to people that it's going to emerge from very nontraditional sources and places, like those of you in this room. We're going to have to have a new kind of spiritual leadership. The answer, Brad, it seems to me will come from spiritual leadership, not from political or economic arenas, and not from education, and not from any of the other social constructions that have caused rather than resolved the problem.

BB: I agree. I have been fascinated by this little book, called "A General Theory of Love" that was written by three psychiatrists from California. They are brain physiology experts. This may seem like a sidetrack, but give me a minute or two and you'll see that it's relevant. What they've been studying is how the brain actually works and how the brain evolved. And one of the things that they talk about is that in the evolution of the brain, as we moved from reptile to mammal, two things occurred that were parallel to each other. One was the development of this thin little layer of brain cells over the reptilian brain. It's very thin, but they are different kind of cells from the reptilian brain and it's also different kind of cells from the neocortex.

This little brain happened to develop at the same time we started giving birth to babies instead of laying eggs. Reptiles lay eggs and when they hatch, if the parents happen to be there, they eat the children without any sense of identity or taking care of their own. But when babies started being born out of the body of the mother, there was this parallel development on top of the reptilian brain called the limbic brain. So, currently they say we have three brains: the reptilian brain, the limbic brain and the neocortex.

The limbic brain has to do with taking care of your own, protecting your little babies, not only not eating them yourself but also protecting them from others. So as we developed, our limbic brain developed, and on top of that we developed the neocortex.

One perspective is that we've gone through this long period of history in which, because of the development of the neocortex (through which we've been able to come up with technological advances and ideas and ideals) we generally overrule our hearts with our minds. This happens because we operate out of sets which we developed through thinking (which is a function of the neocortex) and they predominate and control *how we use* feelings of caring. But we also have this continual development of our hearts because we were raised by mothers and fathers and raised in families, and we do find that compassion and spirituality are, in fact, *learned in relation to being cared for* and are a relevant and important aspect of our experience of being here. The question arises, what is the proper function for a human being with these three brains? What leads? Should it actually be the neocortex, or should it be the heart, the limbic brain? The limbic brain, by the way, is literally wired to the sensations around the heart.

NDW: Not coincidentally.

BB: Not coincidentally, no. The limbic sensations are wired into sensations in this (the heart) part of the body. The age-old argument that's been going on for 5,000 years or so, in the writings of the world, is about the conflict between heart and mind. What happens is that people hurt the ones they love occasionally because they go back to their reptilian response or use their neocortex to enhance their immediate-self-interest survivor skills. The question is, what happens then?

What I think happens is you get a skipped-over or limited use of the limbic brain—and your actions reflect primarily the use of your reptilian and neocortical brain—what we might call the militant or military mind. That's what makes military intelligence an oxymoron. It's not that those folks are completely devoid of feeling, it is just usually in the form of a kind of pathetic and usually alcoholic sentimentality, so they'll get all teary-eyed about getting the boys home for Christmas or folding the flag at a funeral, but it doesn't have much influence on the choices they make from within the mindset in which they operate. Like, for example, napalming whole villages. Whereas the person in which the limbic brain, or the feeling in the heart is the primary organizing principle (mostly women, I think, in our culture, and maybe universally) is thoughtful in a different way. These people use their reptilian brain and their neocortex in obedience to their limbic function.

This spring, I'm releasing a book called "Radical Parenting: Seven Steps to a Functional Family in a Dysfunctional World." It is focused on how to raise children to be citizens of the world and to operate based on learning love. It asks, "How do you raise children to develop their limbic capacity to be primary and their intellectual capacity to be secondary?" Most of us weren't raised that way. Many of us were raised with love, but within the intellectual Judeo-Christian mind set in which, actually, the function of the neocortical brain and the mind is given too much primacy.

I think this tends to be true not only in our tradition, but in most of the institutional religious traditions of the world, in which *the words of dead people get more votes than the words of the living.* In the way we were raised, the function of the mind is to figure out what to do and then do it, so the stress is still on *figuring out* and *being morally upright.* Whereas a focus on acting out of caring, as we discussed earlier about the Golden Rule, turns out to be less moralistic and yet more authentically moral.

NDW: What we are talking about here is the new age conversation about body, mind and spirit.

BB: Yes, we're talking about body, mind and spirit. But what the spirit could do, with regard to giving spirit primacy, or having spiritual leaders lead, would definitely change the world. Regardless of what theology people come from, there is a kind of an agreement that if we lead with our feeling for each other, our ability to care for each other, our heart, our spiritual mind, our common unity so to speak, then the way we organize other things, like the economy or business or defense, etc.

would be around that feeling center. If we are doing that, if we were following that spiritual lead—that is what spiritual leadership is.

What seems to defeat spiritual leadership is preoccupation with things that are more concerned with survival. Things like greed, domination, control of property, and those kinds of things, which are really reptilian. (Laughter) We are never going to not have that, of course. We are always going to be greedy. It gets synthesized with protecting the ones we love, but against the other ones of us—those who might harm the ones we love or take something from us. Then we are off to the races and the cops and robbers game is on again. Current reactions to the September 11th tragedy are a good example. People are waving flags and playing "God Bless America" and talking about how we're gonna get 'em back. Some of us will never get past that phase. When some of us do get past that phase, will there be enough of us to determine our direction? Are we going to move more in the direction of being lead by our ability to care for each other or by our desire to destroy the enemy?

NDW: And I assert that our ability to care for each other is directly related to our ability to relate to each other as part of ourselves. It's very difficult for us to care for, ultimately, something to which we do not experience a direct relationship. If it's "over there" and we are "over here" it's very difficult for us to relate to it.

The mindset that could cause what you are describing to happen, is that we could move into our limbic response and begin to care for each other rather than protect ourselves from each other. The mind set that's going to be required is a mindset, as we talked about a while ago, which expands our definition of self, because in the end all interest is self-interest. And the beauty of that is that it closes the circle. The beauty of the model we've described is that it closes the circle from the limbic brain right back down to the reptilian brain. Because when the reptilian brain (and the neocortical brain) understands that it is in its own best self-interest to care for the other, the circle is closed.

BB: Yeah. It's what we call enlightened self-interest. Which is to get that my interest and yours are in alignment.

NDW: So we don't see the reptilian brain, with all the fundamental survival skills of man, and the neocortex with the logic center that helps us arrange and understand all of that, and then the limbic brain telling us that we should all care for each other, as *separate.* We see, rather, all three in deep harmony with each other.

The reptilian brain is responding automatically because the *whole brain now understands* that this other person, place or thing must be cared for and protected, because this other person, place or thing is part of the Self. So the circle gets completed. You've just devised a whole circular construction there.

That closes the gap. We no longer have the reptilians vs. the limbic folk, no longer the left vs. the right. We no longer have the brutes vs. the softies. We suddenly see that, in fact, by simply shifting our awareness of what's so with regard to the other, the two are really working for and struggling for and fighting for the very same thing.

BB: Yeah. It's the kind of unity that we already have, and we simply need to let it be what we operate from.

NDW: Maybe it's the neocortex after all, that needs to say to both of these, "Hey, hey, hey! Are you guys listening to each other? Hello?" (Laughter)

BB: There's a further implication with regard to our concern about ecology. We have to recognize that the beings that we used to think of, when we were cavemen—animals we thought of as our enemies, you know, like the beasts in Jurassic Park—are also us. They are us, too. In the sense that if we need to maintain our forests and keep a variety of species, regardless of whether they'd eat us or not if they had the chance. *All of being is in our self-interest, too.*

Our enlightened self-interest includes the maintenance and care for all of Being. If that is a primary value, upheld, ritualized, and repeated often—and we personally reminded each other of this among a group of spiritual leaders who come from the heart—or a cabinet made up of people who have some economic and political power as well—then the economic and political structures will have to change, because they're clearly not now consistent with that principle.

So we'd have to have a major change in the economic and political structures, because that's what allows that wholeness to be manifested in the world. There is, among a minority of people, a fairly good degree of awareness of this. Which is why you and I sell a fair number of books and why we can go on tour and why people will come and listen to us. There is a growing awareness that our enlightened self-interest as human beings includes an interest in all of Being.

Our limbic intelligence, or our hearts leading and our minds following, tell us we are the stewards of Being. If we assume then, as a mind set, that we are the stewards of Being, then that tells us what we are primarily supposed to be doing. Then, suddenly the Pentagon budget and foreign policy (and the existence of thirty-six secret agencies where we don't even get to see what they do until many years later) the war on drugs and the poverty, starvation and circumstances of living for billions of human beings, are seen in a different light. We look at the structure of government where there's so much secrecy involved, in a different light. We start looking at a serious issue, one which has been my primary focus in individual, family and community life: the function of secrecy and the results of secrecy. When you hold this perspective as the steward of being (a limbic view which is critical to changing the structures of society) the first thing to come under review is secrecy. What would happen if we said, "Okay, this is everything we have in the CIA files. We're going to declassify all classified documents."

NDW: It's the elimination of secrecy that allows us to eliminate individualized self-interest.

BB: I think so, yes.

NDW: It does, because individualized self-interest would be virtually impossible to express if we were transparent about everything we were thinking saying and doing! By the very nature of transparency, the collective reality is called to the awareness of what each individual is undertaking, attempting and doing, and in that moment even the individualized do-ing becomes a collective experience. So I agree with you profoundly.

I've often asked myself, what does it mean to have anything pri-vate? This leads to a fundamental question. These days we're seeing in the newspapers the following argument: Is the government overreach-ing, going too far with these proposed security measures? Are we losing a modicum of privacy? In life I say, who cares? So what? I'm not threat-ened by Big Brother watching me. Let them watch me all they want.

BB: That's right. I agree. Let them print everything I do in the "Wash-ington Post" every morning, as far as I'm concerned. It'll be fairly boring reading, and it doesn't matter to me. The big problem though, is what *Big Brother* is allowed to keep secret from *us*.

NDW: And if we did that with every organization, every religion, every government, every corporation and everybody knew everything, then suddenly, we would almost automatically act in our mutual self-interest because acting every other way would be—

BB: Stupid.

NDW: Stupid and embarrassing—terribly embarrassing, because everyone would know it! The only thing that allows us to act in an "in-dividualized self-interest" fashion, serving ourselves even to the disser-vice of another, is secrecy! What we like to call privacy. But if there was no such thing as privacy of any kind, then people would start behaving in a way that was aligned with our collective self-interest.

BB: I agree. I have a lot of couples in groups and couples therapy who talk about how they don't want to tell each other everything be-cause they believe it will take the romance out of the relationship, be-cause the mystery is what allows for the romance. I say them over and over again, "There's plenty of mystery, don't worry. I think you can reveal everything you can possibly reveal and there will still be an immense mystery." And the little teeny mysteries you preserve by withholding are more likely to be blocks to your contact with each other than they are to be something that contributes to romance. Romantic idealism is a long way from love. There's plenty of mystery out there without having to be so self-protected and so self-interested.

NDW: My most romantic moments, by the way, were moments when I chose not to withhold anything. That's the point you're making. The most thrilling exciting moments of my life, whether romantically, sexually, or in any other kind of contact way, was when I simply sat down and laid all my cards on the table.

I recall meeting a woman years ago at a party and I looked right at her and said, "I want to go to bed with you. Sorry I've put it that way, but I've only got about five minutes here." And she said, "I wouldn't mind doing that with you, either." And that was the most exciting weekend either of us had ever had. We told each other everything and neither one of us had ever experienced that before. We asked ourselves at the end of that weekend: Why can't we just do this all the time? By the way, we have never seen each other again since, and we knew that we probably wouldn't. We live in two different worlds from two different parts of the country.

But we sat there at the end of that extraordinarily exciting weekend and said to each other, "Why do you suppose it happened like this?" We agreed that the reason it happened was probably because we decided from the first minute we saw each other that there was no time for game playing. We knew that if anything delicious was going to occur, it would have to be out of a space of total transparency, complete honesty, and utter openness with each other. So we went to that, and it was a delicious, delicious experience.

BB: I know it. It happens a lot when you're on the road. It happened to me frequently when I took a year off and went on a trip around the world with just a backpack and a guitar. I think it's partly because when people travel, and are removed from their usual context at home and they are not worried about who's going to find out or what people are going to think, they can be less defensive. So they open up and are honest.

One thing that would serve to expand each human being's identification with humanity, would be to just send all of us around the world. What if we had some kind of travel program so that everyone in the world got to travel some? What if we took a government budget and said we were going to get everybody in the world to get to visit somewhere else in the world? We could take our tremendous ability to provide transportation and say, okay, America, take August off, and you get to go to China.

NDW: Great! (Laughter)

BB: There's some kind of way that our expanded awareness of each other would be served. The Internet helps some, TV helps some. I think there are so many other things that can be productively focused on besides defense, that would allow for this expanded identification with each other, and with all of Being.

If we keep that as the primary focus for action—and it clearly is our primary focus, all your books are about it, all my books are about it, all my seminars are about it, all your seminars are about it—what we're talking about is the ability for suffering humanity to experience the joyfulness that we've had the opportunity to experience, by virtue of not being limited to merely mirroring our defensiveness. I mean, I've been plenty defensive in my life, plenty of times. We have plenty of experiences of that, too. But, like you said, the most delightful moments, with your kids, with your lovers, with your friends, are moments where you're not defended.

There's a great new book, "Undefended Love" by Jett Psaris and Marlena Lyons. I have e-mailed back and forth with Jett some. It's a great book about non-defensiveness. By the way, I told her I'd like for her to be Secretary of Defense in our Cabinet because of her book "Undefended Love." She said fine, she would be Secretary of Defense!

NDW: So Brad, where do we go from here? In the aftermath of the September 11 attacks and all the events that followed, where do we go from here? What is appropriate for us to say to the American public and the world at large about where we go from here and how do we get there?

BB: Well, the first thing to be said is what we've said already. We pay attention to how we organize ourselves and use our resources and check out whether what we're doing is done in defense of some lesser definition of self, or about one that is all inclusive.

NDW: It's what Thich Nhat Hanh calls mindful consumption.

BB: Yeah, or the new bottom line that Michael Lerner speaks of. Let's say we're all on a boat and we have a limited amount of food. I take a bite and give you a bite, and it doesn't make any difference whether I bought it or not. We share what we have so we all can live longer. It's like *Mi casa es su casa.* Some kind of idea of my house is your house, but for the whole world.

NDW: Or, what I do for you I do for me. And what I fail to do for you I fail to do for me. And the question is, how do we get from where we are to where we want to be?

BB: Well, if we developed a primary screening device, what items would be on the list? First of all, question one we would ask, "Is this truly in our enlightened self-interest as human beings?" That's screening device number one.

NDW: Or something that is redefined as in our collective best interest. Is it in the best interest of the largest number of people, as defined by them? Is that what you'd say?

BB: I don't know. This issue comes up for me over and over again about whether or not I trust democracy. We're talking about an elitism already. We're saying we're going to get a whole bunch of thought leaders to be on this cabinet. We've got to recognize that there are people who do know more than other people about Being and the management of the sustenance of Being. There are people who know more about ecology than others and there are people who know more about the limbic brain and so forth. But we have to be able to somehow rely on our experts without surrendering our authority to them. It's the age-old dilemma of democracy.

When you say self-interest "in the opinion of the greatest number of people," I have to admit I don't really trust people to know what is in their enlightened self-interest. If what they say disagrees with my assessment of what I think is in their enlightened self interest, then I think I'm right and they're wrong. I don't trust the majority of people today to be aware of their own enlightened self-interest. There is a lot to be learned out there for all of us.

NDW: Isn't that a function of leadership?

BB: Well, say more. Yes, probably.

NDW: Aren't leaders those who have the ability, the will, the desire and the facility to speak to the masses, if you please, and cause the largest number of people to understand what is truly so? That's what made the Christs, the Lincolns, the Gandhis? And isn't that what we are lacking in this part of our human history? We don't have that one or two or three or five . . .

BB: Yes! Even that has to be a collective! It may be this body we're imagining we're calling the cabinet to get ready for the 2004 elections.

NDW: Eloquent spokespersons. Eloquent people who can articulate in ways that everyone can understand what is so. In fact, then the democracy agrees democratically. It's no longer the brains of the few dictating to the minds of the many. In fact, it's the minds of the many *clearly understanding,* because it's been placed before them in such a way that they can't miss it and the largest number of people suddenly agree.

It's a function of leadership, and that's what we're lacking in this period of history. We do not have enough of these eloquent spokespersons. It's sad, because at a time when communication is so easy, so widespread, and when it's possible to reach the entire human race, we do not have enough message-senders. We have a dearth of message-senders when we have a huge surplus, a plethora, of communication opportunities and abilities. If we had a Lincoln today . . .

BB: Well, it can't be entirely up to just the most eloquent speakers. When concepts are substituted for experiences, we are always in danger of giving our authority to the best, most eloquent speaker. And, what about Hitler? People who stir people are fine, but there needs to be a spread of shared vested authority. That's why we attempted to structure shared power in constituting the United States, rather than having simple obedience to either the loudest or most articulate leader.

I think the time for external leadership by one great articulator is probably over anyway. If we are a *group* of leaders who point people back into their experience and we're providing examples by how we live, modeling how others might take a stand from within their own individual enlightened realm of experience, a real paradigm shift will occur because more people will "get" it than ever before. Leaders who exemplify how to be led by their hearts, because they are able to act together—leaders in accord with their hearts and working out what to do together—show the way.

That, of course, is what real democracy is. Maybe we should call it Limbic Democracy. But, wait a minute; maybe we do have that in this vision we are discussing! What if we got together this group of people, and we say we're willing to serve in these various appointed capacities, and that we're going to be interviewing candidates and select one to be spokesperson for this value? We start interviewing people who want to run for president, and people we would like to see run. I like Oprah. We call Oprah and we say: "We want someone who can appeal to a large number of people, who is well-known and who has compassion. We need someone whose heart is in the right place and who will help us communicate to people that we can and need to reorganize the world consistent with values that are in our enlightened self-interest just as you and I have talked about. We think you qualify. We want to talk to you to see if you are the person."

So we become a sort of kitchen cabinet of leaders to select the leadership for ourselves. We focus all of our attention on the leaders who can do the best job of articulating to the masses the possibility of *making it all up differently.*

If we start doing that we can learn a lot and we can teach prospective candidates, whoever they may be, through this process.

NDW: We have some highly articulate, highly motivated and deeply compassionate communicators on the planet right now. People who can articulate in a sentence or two with great clarity what's going on, what's up and what we can do to change it; people who have terrifically powerful ideas about reorganizing the world. Michael Lerner is one. You're another. Louise Diamond, who wrote "The Peace Book," is a third. Marianne Williamson is yet one more. She can get on Oprah and in thirty seconds say it. She's got thirty-seven seconds and she doesn't even need all thirty-seven. She's an extraordinarily articulate person and she's got a mind that's able to collect her thoughts, express them and articulate them very quickly in a way that people get. They just get it.

There are others, many others. All people who can say in a paragraph or two what needs to be said in a way that causes the average person to read it and say, "Yup, I get that. Maybe I don't get all the stuff in that foreign policy book, but I get that. I get that."

That's what we need, people who, when they speak, produce what I call big "gets." Big gets.

BB: I like that. I get it.

NDW: I'll tell you one thing, if Oprah didn't want to run for President I'd suggest Marianne Williamson, because she has the ability to articulate very important ideas very quickly, in a moment, with twenty-five words or less. She'd win any contest where you had to answer, in twenty-five words or less the question: What do we need to do to save the world? And she'll give you twenty-two words that'll knock your socks off. Barbara Marx Hubbard needs to be in that group, too. In the cabinet. I think we ought to have a new cabinet department dealing with the future. We don't have a futurist. Secretary of the Future. We don't have that and we need future builders.

BB: That's Barbara Marx Hubbard!

NDW: That's absolutely Barbara Marx Hubbard.

BB: Secretary of the Future.

NDW: We need to have that.

BB: That's so much better than "Homeland Defense."

NDW: That was a very poor, unfortunate choice of words.

BB: I think so.

NDW: As soon as I saw it I thought, oh, no! And we embraced that and accepted it. Nobody said, "Ummm, can we find another name please?" But Secretary of the Future. Yes. And I'll tell you someone else who's articulate and marvelous at expressing quickly and profoundly the kind of truths that we need to understand, and that's Jean Huston. Her book "Jump Time" is a work of genius.

So, interestingly enough, we have all these women. A group that would include people like Jean Huston, Barbara Marx Hubbard, and Marianne Williamson would be unbelievably powerful in creating, synthesizing and sending a message to the world. We're seeing some very, very powerful women emerging now in the front line of spiritual and philosophical leadership, if not political leadership, in this country.

BB: And it is about time. They are more likely to be limbically attuned and articulate and brilliant and we'll be needing need more women than men in government for a century or so anyway, to bring about a little balance. Reintegrating the feminine in men and having women in formerly male world leadership positions is very similar work. It is a core element of our ability to heal the world. Especially since we macho men, by and large, in our ignorance and our false sense of separation, are so committed to war ourselves into oblivion in the name of survival, no matter how many women and children we have to kill in the process.

Well, let's do it. Let's organize this kitchen cabinet and ask them. This could be really exciting!

NDW: Yeah, it could! And it would be "upheavaling," too, to coin a word. The time begs for leadership. The time begs for someone to step out. It begs for it because all of our presently-in-place institutions have let us down, as I see it. They have let us down. We're even afraid to admit that, and I understand that. If we look at all those institutions and acknowledge that they have let us down, we think, now where do we go? Now what? Where to from here?

Those institutions served their purpose and, given the limited consciousness with which they were created, they were probably in some ways very effective and I'm not making them wrong. But this is a new time and a new day and we need a new way. I've been saying that part of what we need is a new God. This is shaking people up a little bit.

BB: Uh huh, yes. I can imagine.

NDW: This my shorthand way of saying we need a new set of values, from our idea of divinity right on down from what we think divinity is all about, to what we think everything *beneath* that is all about. Just a whole new prime thought that topples the dominoes and creates a new collection of what you call sub-sets and sub-thoughts and what "Conversations with God" calls "sponsoring thoughts." We need a new sponsoring thought.

I was in Danbury, Connecticut not long ago and raised some eyebrows when I said that religion has let us down. That made the headlines. Stories about my appearances around the country generally make page thirty-two (if they get into the paper at all) under a headline that says "Author Appears in Danbury." This story made third page. Open the first page and there it is: "Author Says Religions Have Let Us Down."

Well, now I know how to get near the front page!

BB: What about actually running for the vice-presidency? I mean, actually. You've got the energy for it? Could you do that? I think you're a very articulate spokesperson.

NDW: Probably not. I need to be Secretary of Spirituality or something.

BB: Secretary of Spirituality! God, these are such great categories. We've got to write this down. Oh, we *are* writing this down. (Laughter)

NDW: You see, these are the areas of our lives we're not paying attention to, that we're not actively creating. We say that we're a spiritual nation, we even call ourselves "one nation under God," and yet we don't have any secretary of spirituality who enhances and defends and creates and constructs and articulates the spiritual undergirding that presumably supports everything this country stands for and everything it does. Who's articulating that? We don't have that.

We have Billy Graham and in the last forty-five years he's been the ex-officio secretary of spirituality for this country and God bless him, he's done the best he could. He slowly made his way up there to the pulpit at the national memorial service . . .

BB: I saw that. I appreciated him for that. My heart went out to him.

NDW: Absolutely. Got himself out of his house at, I'm sure, considerable discomfort to play, once again, the nation's pastor. A little tear came down my cheek and I thought, "Well, God bless him for showing up."

But, Billy can't do it any more. It's someone else's time. But we don't have any more leaders like Billy Graham, or Bishop Fulton Sheen, or the Rev. Norman Vincent Peale. Who do we have on the national religious scene of that stature?

Besides, it's not about yesterday's religious doctrines anyway. We've got to transcend those. Not discard them, but *use* them and move *through* them to a larger spirituality that includes our experience of them, but produces a grander view of human possibilities and divine realities.

BB: Well, good. This is it. This is what we're talking about in this cabinet and that would be your proper function as spiritual leader. I would like for Pema Chödrön to be there with you and for you all to have Thich Nhat Hanh and the Dalai Lama as frequent consultants. Wouldn't it be great to have two people for each of these posts? We could have a couple for each one! A couple could be Secretary of Defense, have a couple be President, have a couple be Vice-President. Of course, then we'd be doing couples therapy all the time. (Laughter)

NDW: What you'd have then is the yin and the yang, the left and the right, the male and the female of it. You'd have both of those energies having an effect on decisions and policies and articulations.

BB: You know, the Senate was created for this country actually based on the model of the Grandmother's Council that the Iroquois invented. The grandmothers were the second approving body besides the warriors, and approval by both groups was required before action could be taken. The Grandmother's Council is what eventually evolved into our Senate. I think we should go back to having a Grandmother's Council.

NDW: It would be fun to find some way to pull this together, but I think there are some practical things, these musings apart and aside, that real people can do in the real world to produce a real difference, right here, right now. And what I have been saying to people as I travel the country and the world is, for God's sake, *take a leadership position.*

If you're only the head council of your own family group, *take a leadership position.* I keep trying to articulate that opportunity, that this is the open moment for each of us to step into, assuming real leadership within the sphere of our own influence. We can all become Centers of Influence. Each of us are COIs. When we are willing to assume that profile, that's when the shift in consciousness that we need will come and when the changes that we pray for will be made.

BB: People in New York have told us that they are all closer now. They are kinder to each other than New Yorkers used to be. All over America we have this experience, this sense of all being in the same boat.

I hear people saying things like, "Oh, you know that person I didn't want to talk to? Well, I'm willing to talk to them now." Or, "Well, you know that ex I hate? Well, I'm willing to make up with them now." I think that's the place to start.

NDW: We can start in our own lives to finish what Elisabeth Kübler-Ross calls our unfinished business. A good place to start to help yourself and your world is with your own unfinished business.

BB: Who do you need to forgive? Who have you been hiding from? Lying to? Holding something against? You can't have peace in the world without peace in your life. It's impossible. Where else would you start but with yourself? The structures can't transform until enough individuals transform first. It's impossible to do it the other way around. So get out there and finish your unfinished business. Great.

That's great stuff, great advice for all of us. And that's a great place to end this book. Let's just all decide we're going to do that. We're going to finish with our unfinished business, we're going to move to a new level of honesty with each other, and practice radical honesty as a lifestyle, and we're going to change the world with this. We're going to change the world that we touch, and that's going to spread and change the world at large.

NDW: I'm with you. I'm for that. Let's GO.

The Mother of All Postscripts

We know that one thing that can heal us of the sadness, the injury, the damage, the sense of hurt and the experience of impotence that many people have, is to give ourselves something to do. That's true in any healing situation, even a death. That's why we all do what we do around funerals. We give parties and put the food out and talk to each other about the person who passed. It's all about healing. It's something we can do.

When you bring a casserole over to the house, you feel like you've done something and your sadness is, to that degree, diminished. And your sense of damage is diminished, because you're able to "be" in a way which serves and activates your higher thought about who you are.

So one thing that we can all create is something to be and do right now to diminish our sense of impotence in the face of this awful, terrible feeling of fear, loss of security and tragedy that the human race is enduring. To the degree that we give ourselves something viable and possible, we can heal ourselves.

● ● ●

BB: It definitely helps to go to work creating. What I'm wondering is whether we should create some kind of website in order for us to organize. Then keep the conversation going.

NDW: We should do that. We should create a way for those of us who want to build a new tomorrow, to make a brighter future, can join together in doing that.

BB: Okay. Let's establish a site at changeofheart.biz, and set it up so that people can dialogue with us to get information and ideas about all that they can do to help shift humanity's collective reality. We'll have our slate of candidates and our proposed cabinet up there, too, for discussion.

NDW: There are many programs that we can point to, as well. For instance, I've already formed through the ReCreation Foundation, which sponsors the work of CWG Centers around the world, an action movement called OnenessNow. The longer name for it is Oneness Now Everywhere, which is O-N-E, of course. Bumper stickers and window stickers are being manufactured even as we sit here and speak. We're inviting people all over the world to join Oneness Now by going to www.onenessnow.com

What I'm proclaiming is that we could put an end to all of this with a single idea, and in my articulation that is called "oneness." What we need is oneness now everywhere. In our politics, in our economics, in our education, in our religion.

This does not mean "sameness," but it does mean "unity." Even as the fingers on a hand are not the same, but are part of one body, so can the unity of humankind be experienced and expressed through our human institutions, without anyone having to give up their individuality.

And so we've established very quickly this OnenessNow program, and put it in place. The website's already up at www.OnenessNow.com, and we're issuing a call for people to join us. There's no membership fee. We do offer people who wish to do so the opportunity to assist financially, but it is not required. The idea is that this organization will produce, at the grassroots level, a cadre of people in every city, town and village who are prepared now to sit down together, to dialogue, to work with each other in producing local-level action programs to bring us all together in a common experience of our humanity.

We'll be working with these local groups to suggest unifying activities and undertakings related to the local economy, to local politics, to local education, and to local spiritual and religious organizations and movements. We're giving assignments like, go to your community and organize a dialogue group of all the interfaith ministers, and report back to us when you've done that. In Miami we already had one. The CWG Center there had forty ministers from all the faiths sitting down and dialoguing with all the Muslims, the Jews, the Catholics, the Protestants and all the rest, sitting around a table saying, what can we do? What can we do here in Miami to affect and communicate with the faith community with regard to what is going on? What can we tell our congregations is the appropriate spiritual response, given our different spiritual perspectives? What does that look like to us? They had a marvelous meeting.

We're giving people specific assignments. There are about twenty assignments, and that's one of them. There is specific stuff we can do in our communities right now to create a larger sense of our oneness. I've already moved ahead, due to my innate impatience.

We'll also be networking with others, connecting people who believe in this concept with like-minded groups and organizations, such as the Global Renaissance Alliance (RenaissanceAlliance.com) and your own nation whose borders are the atmosphere of the earth, the United States of Being (usob.org).

BB: Okay. So this is a call to action to all those who may be reading this, and who agree with what's been said here. The first step is for you to log on to www.changeofheart.biz and pick up the information that we'll continually make available there.

This site will be where we organize the selection and volunteering of compassionate leaders to be the cabinet for a candidate for the presidential elections in 2004. It will also be where we track the conversation about actions we can all take to create unity in the world. It will also be a networking point for connection to all the other sites we now operate and know of and can find, whose participants and sponsors are leaders in this transformation to a new bottom line.

Those without an Internet connection may write to:

CHANGE OF HEART
646 Shuler Lane
Stanley, VA 22851

Or they may call 1-800-EL TRUTH.

NDW: One thing we have to make clear. People should not do this in order to help us. We're not setting this up in order for us to get help with something that *we* want to do. The purpose of this is to help *others* do something that *they* want to do.

This is a chance for people to announce and declare Who They Really Are in the face of the events now taking place throughout the world. Every act is an act of self-definition. This is about defining yourself. This is everyone's Declaration of Independence. Independence from fear of terrorist attacks, from all forms of corporate and government manipulation, from control, from oppression (subtle and otherwise), from dogma and dishonesty, and from all the negative forces that seek to influence human beings.

Robert Kennedy said that there are those who see the world as it is and ask, "Why?" And there are those who dream of things that never were, and ask, "Why not?"

This is a chance for us to stand up and say "No, thank you" to those who would seek to count us out, do us in, have us call it quits, or give up our dreams of things that never were.

This is a chance for us to produce, in our own lives and in the lives of all those we touch, a change of heart that can change the world.

BB: Amen.

www.changeofheart.biz

Appendix

RADICAL HONESTY ENTERPRISES WWW.RADICALHONESTY.COM

Radical Honesty is a kind of communication that is direct, complete, open and expressive. Radical Honesty means you tell the people in your life what you've done or plan to do, what you think, and what you feel. It's the kind of authentic sharing that creates the possibility of love and intimacy.

What we DO:

We publish books and conduct seminars. We conduct the Power of Honesty Workshop (three days, one evening) the Course in Honesty (eight days, residential) and the workshop called Honesty in the World (five days, residential, requires previous participation in one of the above two workshops). The practice of Radical Honesty is based on the work and writings of Dr. Brad Blanton, a psychologist who found that the best way to reduce stress, make life work, and heal the past was to tell the truth.

THE CENTER FOR RADICAL HONESTY

The Center for Radical Honesty is a non-profit corporation in Virginia, in the United States. Contributions are tax deductible and the money contributed goes to support scholarships for seminars for people for whom it is difficult find the money to pay for the programs, and for special programs of the Center, like "The Thought Leaders Course in Honesty." To find out more, write us at:

The Center for Radical Honesty
646 Shuler Lane
Stanley, VA 22851
Or call for more information (540) 778 3488.

THE BOOKS ARE:

"Radical Honesty: How to Transform Your Life by Telling the Truth"

"Practicing Radical Honesty: How to Complete the Past, Live in the Present and Build a Future with a Little Help from Your Friends"

"Radical Parenting: How to Have a Functional Family in a Dysfunctional World"

"The Truthtellers: Stories of Success by Honest People"

OUR MISSION

At Radical Honesty Enterprises we are building communities of intimate friends who are creating a revolution in consciousness through direct, open and honest conversation. What's in it for me?

People who practice Radical Honesty have healthy, free, powerful and joyful lives. Lying and protecting your image takes a heavy toll on your health and relationships. Telling the truth is less destructive than lying.

HOW CAN I FIND OUT MORE?

Check out the latest issue of our newsletter, "The Radical Honesty eZine" at www.radicalhonesty.com

Online Audio and Video—Listen to Brad talk about Radical Honesty and read from his book at www.radicalhonesty.com

Read the first and last chapters of Brad's book "Practicing Radical Honesty: How to Complete the Past, Stay in the Present, and Build a Future With a Little Help From Your Friends" at www.radicalhonesty.com

Online, read the first two chapters of the book "Radical Honesty: How to Transform Your Life by Telling the Truth."

We call upon all caring people to sign the Declaration of Independence for a New Millennium and help through ongoing participation to form a new nation. We expect people who are engaged in recovery, the personal growth movement, and people who are just plain fed up, to be our core group and we expect damn near everyone else to join us as they come to understand the truth of what we have to say. Our objective is to organize a new government for a new nation, to be built first in our imaginations and in cyberspace after we sign up as citizens by signing the new Declaration of Independence. We then intend to grow larger as a political force in the current structure at the same time we model a new one, and then take over increasingly the actual functions of government. We call our new country the United States of Being and we intend it to be based on the sovereignty of the individual, rather than the sovereignty of the king, or the sovereignty of representatives. Contact our web site at www.usob.org and sign the Declaration of Independence for the New Millennium and become a member of the United States of Being.

September 1, 1939

By W. H. Auden

I sit in one of the dives
On Fifty-second Street
Uncertain and afraid
As the clever hopes expire
Of a low dishonest decade:
Waves of anger and fear
Circulate over the bright
And darkened lands of the earth,
Obsessing our private lives;
The unmentionable odour of death
Offends the September night.

Accurate scholarship can
Unearth the whole offence
From Luther until now
That has driven a culture mad,
Find what occurred at Linz,
What huge imago made

A psychopathic god:
I and the public know
What all schoolchildren learn,
Those to whom evil is done
Do evil in return.

Exiled Thucydides knew
All that a speech can say
About Democracy,
And what dictators do,
The elderly rubbish they talk
To an apathetic grave;
Analysed all in his book,
The enlightenment driven away,
The habit-forming pain,
Mismanagement and grief:
We must suffer them all again.

Into this neutral air
Where blind skyscrapers use
Their full height to proclaim
The strength of Collective Man,
Each language pours its vain
Competitive excuse:
But who can live for long
In an euphoric dream;
Out of the mirror they stare,
Imperialism's face
And the international wrong.

Faces along the bar
Cling to their average day:
The lights must never go out,
The music must always play,
All the conventions conspire
To make this fort assume
The furniture of home;

Lest we should see where we are,
Lost in a haunted wood,
Children afraid of the night
Who have never been happy or good.

The windiest militant trash
Important Persons shout
Is not so crude as our wish:
What mad Nijinsky wrote
About Diaghilev
Is true of the normal heart;
For the error bred in the bone
Of each woman and each man
Craves what it cannot have,
Not universal love
But to be loved alone.

From the conservative dark
Into the ethical life
The dense commuters come,
Repeating their morning vow;
"I will be true to the wife,
I'll concentrate more on my work,"
And helpless governors wake
To resume their compulsory game:
Who can release them now,
Who can reach the deaf,
Who can speak for the dumb?

All I have is a voice
To undo the folded lie,
The romantic lie in the brain
Of the sensual man-in-the-street
And the lie of Authority
Whose buildings grope the sky:
There is no such thing as the State
And no one exists alone;

Hunger allows no choice
To the citizen or the police;
We must love one another or die.

Defenseless under the night
Our world in stupor lies;
Yet, dotted everywhere,
Ironic points of light
Flash out wherever the Just
Exchange their messages:
May I, composed like them
Of Eros and of dust,
Beleaguered by the same
Negation and despair,
Show an affirming flame.